Editing Texts From the Age of Erasmus

Editing Texts From the Age of Erasmus

Papers given at the
Thirtieth Annual Conference
on Editorial Problems
University of Toronto,
4–5 November 1994

Edited by Erika Rummel

UNIVERSITY OF TORONTO PRESS
Toronto Buffalo London

© University of Toronto Press Incorporated 1996
Toronto Buffalo London
Printed in Canada

ISBN 0-8020-0797-X

Printed on acid-free paper

Canadian Cataloguing in Publication Data

Conference on Editorial Problems (30th : 1994 :
University of Toronto)
Editing texts from the age of Erasmus : papers
given at the thirtieth annual conference on Editorial
Problems, University of Toronto, 4–5 November 1994

ISBN 0-8020-0797-X

1. Literature, Modern – 15th and 16th centuries –
Congresses. 2. Literature, Modern – 15th and 16th
centuries – Translations – Congresses. 3. Archival
materials – Editing – Congresses. 4. Editing –
Congresses. 5. Criticism, Textual – Congresses.
I. Rummel, Erika, 1942– . II. Title.

PN162.C6 1994   808'.02   C95-932652-9

University of Toronto Press acknowledges
the financial assistance to its publishing program
of the Canada Council and the Ontario Arts Council.

Contents

Notes on Contributors

Erika Rummel is Associate Professor of History at Wilfrid Laurier University, Waterloo. She is a member of the Editorial Board of *The Collected Works of Erasmus* and a contributor to several volumes in that edition. She is Secretary of the Erasmus of Rotterdam Society and Chair of Publications of the Renaissance Society of America. She has written several books on Erasmus, most recently *Erasmus and His Catholic Critics* (Nieuwkoop 1989) and edited a collection of Reformation satires, *Scheming Papists and Lutheran Fools* (New York 1993). Her latest monograph is *The Humanist-Scholastic Debate in the Renaissance and Reformation* (Cambridge, Mass. 1995). A collection of texts, *Erasmus On Women*, is forthcoming from University of Toronto Press.

James K. Farge is a Senior Fellow at the Pontifical Institute of Medieval Studies, Toronto; previously he was Professor of History at the University of St Thomas, Houston. He is the author of *Orthodoxy and Reform in Early Reformation France* (Leiden 1985); editor of *Registre des procès-verbaux de la Faculté de Théologie* (Paris 1990), of *Index de l'Université de Paris, 1544–1556* (with F. Higman and J.-M. Bujanda), and *Le Parti conservateur au XVI siècle: Université et Parlement de Paris à l'époque de la Renaissance et de la Réforme* (Paris 1990). He is past chair of the Editorial Committee of *Medieval Studies* and a member of the Editorial Board of *The Collected Works of Erasmus*.

Robert M. Kingdon is Hilldale Professor and Member of the Institute for Research in the Humanities at the University of Wisconsin-Madison. He is on the editorial board of several publications, among them the *Sixteenth Century Journal*. He has compiled, together with J.P. Donnelly, *A Bibliography of the Works of Peter Martyr Vermigli*

(Kirksville 1991); he is the editor of Jean de Coras, *Question politique: s'il est licite aux subjects de capituler avec leur prince* (Geneva 1989), and (with J.-F. Bergier) of *Registres de la Compagnie des Pasteurs de Genève au temps de Calvin,* 2 vols (Geneva 1962, 1964); he is the author of *Myths about the St. Bartholomew's Day Massacres, 1572–1576* (Cambridge, Mass. 1988). In recent years he has been organizing a team to edit the registers of the Geneva Consistory (1542–1564).

J. Daniel Kinney is Associate Professor of English at the University of Virginia. He is the Executive Editor of *Yale Graduate/Professional;* editor and translator of volume 15 and collaborator on volume 3 of *The Complete Works of St Thomas More* (New Haven 1984 and 1986). His edition and translation of *Naufragium ioculare* is forthcoming in the Delaware edition of Abraham Cowley's *Complete Works.*

Anne M. O'Donnell is Associate Professor of English at Catholic University, Washington. She was the convener of the conference 'William Tyndale: Church, State and Word,' held in July 1994 at Catholic University and the Folger Shakespeare Library, Washington; she has edited a special issue of *Moreana* on 'Biblical Interpretation in the Age of Thomas More' (1991); the text of Erasmus' *Enchiridion militis Christiani* (Oxford 1981); and she is the editor of *An Answer unto Sir Thomas More's Dialogue,* forthcoming in the edition of *The Independent Works of William Tyndale* (Catholic University of America Press).

Joseph C. McLelland is McConnell Professor of Philosophy of Religion (emeritus) at McGill University, Montreal; previously he was Robert Professor at the Presbyterian College, Montreal. He has been or is serving on a number of editorial boards: *The Canadian Journal of Theology, Studies in Religion, Theology Today, Blackwell Encyclopedia of Medieval, Renaissance, and Reformation Christian Thought.* He is the author of *Life, Early Letters and Eucharistic Writings of Peter Martyr* (Appleford 1989) and *Peter Martyr Vermigli and Italian Reform* (Waterloo 1980). He is General Editor of the *Peter Martyr Library* (forthcoming from Sixteenth Century Journal Publishers).

James K. McConica is Fellow of All Souls College, Oxford; previously he was a Senior Fellow of the Pontifical Institute of Medieval Studies, Toronto, and President of St Michael's College, University of Toronto. In the past he was joint editor (with Natalie Davis) of *Renaissance and Reformation,* editor of and contributor to *History of the University of Oxford* (volume 3, Oxford 1986), and author of a biography, *Erasmus* (Oxford 1991). He is Chair of the Editorial Board of *The Collected Works of Erasmus* and has annotated volumes 3 and 4 in that edition (Toronto 1976 and 1977). He is also a member of the International Council for the Complete Edition of the Works of Erasmus (Amsterdam).

ERIKA RUMMEL

Introduction

The thirtieth Conference on Editorial Problems, 'Editing Texts from the Age of Erasmus,' took place in Toronto on 4–5 November 1994. The papers presented allowed reflection on successfully completed projects – the editions of the registers of the Faculty of Theology at the University of Paris, the registers of the Company of Pastors of Geneva in the time of Calvin, and *The Complete Works of St Thomas More*; they encouraged exploration of new initiatives – the *Independent Works of Tyndale*, the records of the Consistory of Geneva, and the *Peter Martyr Library*; and they provided an occasion for stock-taking in two ongoing projects – the *Opera Omnia Des. Erasmi* published at Amsterdam and *The Collected Works of Erasmus* published at Toronto. Three of the multi-volume projects were in preparation when the first conference in this series was launched in 1965. At that time the convener, Richard Schoeck, commented on the appropriateness of the conference theme, 'Editing Sixteenth Century Texts,' 'for currently there is considerable editorial activity among sixteenth-century scholars: the More Edition at Yale ... the forthcoming editions of Erasmus, projected work on the reformers.'[1] It is fitting on the thirtieth anniversary of the foundation of the series that the speakers should return to the theme of the first conference and, like Janus, 'looking at once backward and forward,'[2] consider what has been accomplished and what needs to be done. Participants in the 1994 conference could take collective satisfaction in the progress made in the intervening years. The More edition – a daunting project when outlined by its General Editor, the late Richard Sylvester, in the opening address of the first conference – has been practically completed. The two Erasmus projects, barely conceptualized in 1965, have yielded a rich crop of texts and, as James McConica indicates in the concluding paper, are vigorously pursuing their goals in spite of diminishing financial support and shifting priorities at funding agencies. The conference was given encouraging reports, moreover, on the preparation and realization of projects that were only a distant vision when Schoeck spoke of future 'work on the reformers.'

One of the purposes of the conference was to pool intellectual resources, facilitate an exchange of ideas, and initiate discussion that might lead to the solution of shared editorial problems; another was to communicate the findings to a larger scholarly public. The first purpose was achieved in a highly satisfactory degree through the stimulating and productive discussions following individual papers; the second is achieved with the present publication. Its significance lies not only in the transmission of knowledge and expertise, but also in its historiographical function. The speakers offered valuable insights into the nature and process of scholarly collaboration and informed comment on the circumstances that allow such endeavours to flourish. Their remarks, often autobiographical in character, are of intrinsic value to the chronicler of scholarship. Providing a permanent record, the conference proceedings safeguard what would otherwise remain ephemeral oral history.

The papers in this volume appear in the order in which they were presented at the conference. The first two papers treat of archival material, the remainder of literary texts. The arrangement within the categories is chronological. It was thought, however, that the paper on Erasmus deserved a special place. It is unique in offering a comparison between two parallel projects and forms an appropriate conclusion to a conference which acknowledges in its title the seminal influence of Erasmus' works on his age.

In the first paper presented, James Farge spoke of his larger purpose in editing the registers of the Faculty of Theology at Paris. He was motivated by the need to right the balance of scholarly opinion, which at present favours humanists over scholastics. As Farge observes, this predilection or prejudice stems partly from the fact that our age identifies more readily with the despisers of the status quo, partly from the fact that the humanists used language effectively. As a result, a representative number of their writings is available in modern editions and translations, while those of their opponents are not. The publication of the Paris registers is a step in the direction of providing scholars with a more solid base for casting their votes in the humanist-scholastic debate.

Similar considerations prompted Robert Kingdon to organize an edition of the registers of the Geneva Consistory, until now available only in a flawed copy of selected records. Kingdon, like Farge, expressed misgivings about the inaccessibility of the primary sources and about the validity of findings based on imperfect transcriptions and random selection of evidence.

Anne O'Donnell's remarks were closely related to the concerns voiced by the first two speakers. Editing Tyndale's *Answer to More*, for example, meant supplying readers with 'the other half' of the argument at the centre of the polemic and preventing the 'gravitational pull of Sir Thomas More ... from distorting Tyndale's orbit.'[3] Similar considerations were advanced by Daniel Kinney, the editor and translator of More's programmatic letters to Martin Dorp, Edward Lee, and A Monk. These texts provide the essential background to the controversy surrounding the publication of Erasmus' New Testament in 1516. Although the Erasmian argument, which More supports here, has received a great deal of attention in modern scholarship, More's three-pronged attack on the enemies of biblical humanism allows a finer nuancing of interpretations.

Concerns for making available a range of sources representative of a given historical situation and necessary for a fair evaluation constituted a leading theme in the papers presented. Another recurring subject, reflecting recent developments in literary and editorial theory, was the problem of authorship, both in the sense of ascribing a work to a particular author and of discovering the authorial voice in the text. Kinney was one of the speakers addressing this problem. He noted that the texts edited by himself epitomize More's (and more generally speaking, the humanists') ambivalence toward the medium of print and its effect on authorial control. In this context Kinney also discussed the significance of decisions made by the modern editor who, by grouping texts, assigns a generic identity to them. Textual criticism, which determines the definitive shape of a work, is a similarly invasive procedure. Kinney furthermore commented on the marginalized position, literally and conceptually, of modern annotation in spite of its crucial function in uncovering the intricate senses of the text. On a different level, O'Donnell discussed the problem of Tyndale's authorship in collaborative works and the difficulty arising from the concealment of authorship in order to avoid or circumvent censorship. Joseph McLelland pointed out a related problem in editing Peter Martyr's writings. A number of the texts were published posthumously. This creates authorial problems, especially in the lecture notes published by Martyr's disciple John Jewel. If Martyr was diffident about his writings and for this reason refrained from publishing them, the editor overruling the author's misgivings usurps textual control.

The question of what constitutes the authorized version, particularly in aggregated texts, surfaced in several conference papers. It was noted that the two Erasmus editions have chosen radically different approaches in deciding this question. The decisions were influenced in part by the mandate of the editors and the format of the edition. The Amsterdam *Opera*, a critical text for scholars, normally presents the first authorized edition, showing the changes made in later editions in the apparatus. The Toronto edition, an English translation for general readers, uses the last authorized text, which is usually also the fullest version, and restricts itself to indicating important changes in the notes.

In addition to these fundamental questions, speakers also addressed routine matters. Among common problems given an airing were: the difficulty of deciphering manuscript sources and the need for paleographical training; the difficulty of identifying minor historical figures mentioned in the texts; the problem of tracing quotations cited by the author from memory or in variants no longer current; the effort of avoiding Latinate translations and, conversely, of navigating a middle course between producing a smooth, idiomatically correct, modern translation and diverging unduly from the wording of the original.

'Editorial scholarship is no longer an affair for the solitary mortal,' the nineteenth-century classicist John Burnet said.[4] In the concluding paper, James McConica reflected on the cooperative nature of major publishing projects today. He examined the sociology of scholarship, offering as a case study the career of the nineteenth-century Benedictine Germain Morin. It was against this background that McConica viewed the modern 'laborious community'[5] producing the Erasmus editions in Amsterdam and Toronto. Both draw on the expertise of a network of international scholars, an electronically linked *atelier d'érudition*, which has replaced the cloistered community responsible for the learned productions of earlier centuries. McConica drew attention to a number of parallel features in the history of the Toronto and Amsterdam projects, concluding with a poignant account of the convergence of circumstances that brought together the founding committee of ASD. Their shared war experience led them to embrace a new internationalism and deepened their commitment to peace – ideals that are strikingly present in the writings of Erasmus.

The history of CWE likewise has an ideological core. It sprung from a post-war spirit of national enterprise and the courage to make long-term commitments in the expectation of success. Finally, both projects benefited from the vision and staunch support of a scholarly Press willing to give a sympathetic hearing to ambitious plans.

Editing texts remains an important professional task both for the historian and the literary scholar. Making sources accessible to the scholarly public at large is fundamental to continuing research and the development of a historical perspective. A gratifying number of scholars and graduate students from local and regional universities availed themselves of this opportunity to discuss editorial problems and benefit from the expertise of the speakers. Their experience was enhanced by an exhibition of rare books mounted for the duration of the conference by the Centre for Reformation and Renaissance Studies (CRRS) in the rooms of the print museum at Massey College. The display served as a reminder that the holdings of the Centre include one of the best collections of early Erasmus prints on this continent.

The conference committee would like to thank SSHRC, Wilfrid Laurier University, University College in the University of Toronto, and CRRS for their financial support. My thanks also to those who lightened my task as convener: the present and past members of the Committee, especially Germaine Warkentin, from whose experience I have greatly profited; Konrad Eisenbichler, the Director of CRRS, and Joseph Black, its Curator; Marie Korey, the librarian at Massey College; the students at CRRS and at Wilfrid Laurier University, who performed the many mundane, but essential, tasks to ensure the smooth running of the conference; and most particularly, David Galbraith, to whom I am much indebted for his competent handling of the local arrangements. The success of the conference is in large measure due to their contributions.

NOTES

1 *Editing Sixteenth Century Texts* (Toronto 1966) 4
2 The expression is Petrarch's (*Rer. Mem.* 1.19.4).
3 See below 60.
4 Quoted by Richard Schoeck, *Editing Sixteenth Century Texts* 10.
5 Gibbon's term, see below 84.

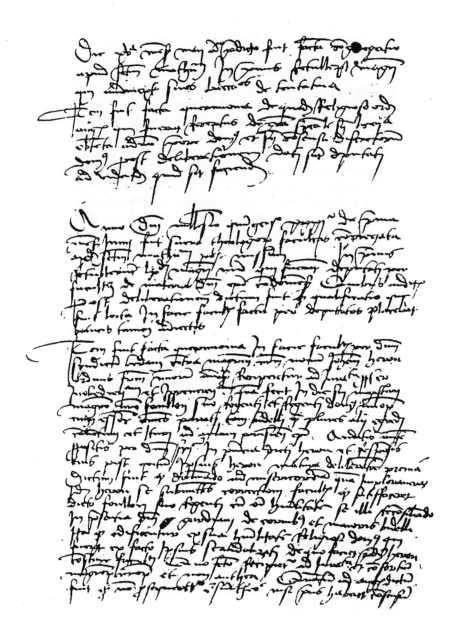

Regestum conclusionum sacrae facultatis theologiae in universitate parisiensi. Paris,
Bibliothèque nationale de France, MS Nouvelles acquisitions latines 1782, f242r

Erasmus manuscript with caricature of Janus. Royal Library of Copenhagen.

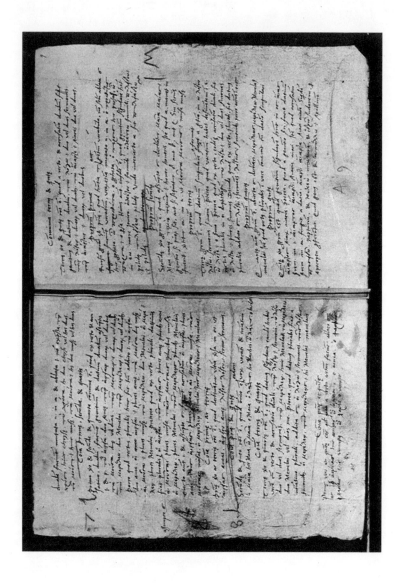

Erasmus manuscript with marginal notes to his translation of the grammar of Theodore of Gaza. University Library of Basel.

Editing Texts From the Age of Erasmus

JAMES K. FARGE

1 Texts and Context of a *Mentalité*: The Parisian University Milieu in the Age of Erasmus

In July 1527, as Desiderius Erasmus was finishing a Latin edition of a Gospel commentary by Origen, he wrote in the preface, 'So vast is the production of new books these days that we run the risk of this profusion becoming an obstacle to learning the truth.' In the same preface he later added, 'There are many things which it would be the height of impiety to call into question today, while in an earlier age inquiry into those same matters constituted religious fidelity.'[1]

It would be easy to interpret Erasmus' statements prima facie as mere criticism of an earlier defective edition of the commentary in question. However, because Erasmus was beset at that time by criticism from every corner of Europe, I believe his words evoke as well two wider preoccupations: first, the glut of books attacking his views and, second, his critics' lack of a sense of historicism. By editing Origen and other Church Fathers Erasmus hoped to redress that imbalance of texts and, at the same time, to demonstrate ways of theologizing which had prevailed prior to the development of scholasticism.

Today, nearly five centuries since Erasmus wrote that preface, the problems he addressed are still with us; but we have managed, as Marx did to Hegel, to stand them on their head. First, the imbalance of texts for one side still exists; but today it heavily favours Erasmus and his humanist-reformist associates. Second, today's 'orthodox' approach to the controversies of the sixteenth century clearly favours Erasmus, and abhors or ignores his scholastic critics. The sheer bulk of his works, the attraction of his rhetoric, the force of his satire, and the surge of interest in humanism and reform have fixed Erasmus firmly in the centre of a constellation of luminaries of the Renaissance and Reformation era. But the corresponding lack of modern editions of texts produced by Erasmus' critics and the conservative establishment, and the general disinclination to research them, should be seen, I think, as a major problem and a challenge for editors of texts and for historians of that era. To have consigned the one group to the limbo of anonymity is perhaps merely careless history. But to make assumptions and draw conclusions without giving equal study to both sides is far more serious, for this skews our understanding of the Age of Erasmus itself.

Let me give an example of the risk of taking Erasmus' rhetoric at face value, without due attention to its context: his famous denunciation of the Collège de Montaigu in the colloquy 'A Fish Diet.' In 1495, Erasmus lived for a year in this Paris college, where the poverty of the place and the ascetic ideals of its founder Jan Standonck proved unbearable to Erasmus' weak constitution and fastidious habits. In the colloquy, Erasmus ruminates a diet of spoiled fish, tainted water, hard bedding, and plaster rotted by nearby latrines.[2] Most readers fail to realize, however, that Erasmus wrote the colloquy almost thirty years later, in 1526, at the height of his campaign to discredit his Parisian critic Noël Beda,[3] whose name was closely tied to Standonck and who had succeeded him in the direction of Montaigu. The colloquy fails to take into account much of what had happened at the college in the intervening thirty years:[4] private and royal philanthropy,[5] new facilities,[6] relaxation of the rigid discipline,[7] and creative pedagogical innovation.[8] Under Beda, in fact, Montaigu became one of the largest and most successful resident colleges,[9] producing many of the University's leading regents.[10] Yet, editors and historians inevitably cite Erasmus and Rabelais, his emulator in this regard,[11] as the last word on the Collège de Montaigu and, by association, on Noël Beda.[12]

In this first part of my presentation, I would like to pursue some thoughts on this ideological imbalance which I have described as both a problem and a challenge for editors of texts from the Age of Erasmus. In the second part, I shall address some concrete problems encountered in my own editorial work.

Editors of sixteenth-century texts have placed at the disposition of historians practically everything that the major and most of the minor humanists and reformers wrote about their visions for change and their hopes for patronage. Their satire of their enemies – the *Letters of Obscure Men* and the *Praise of Folly*, to name the most celebrated – are the commonplaces of the Age. But where today is that plethora of texts[13] about which Erasmus complained, those books by the enemies of change whose beliefs and way of life he targeted with satire and invective? Those men shared not so much a vision of a future as a heritage from the past which they cherished and defended. They too resorted to polemic; but they did so in the *lingua franca* used by educated men for centuries but which had become the butt of ridicule of the humanists. Their letters and texts are not part and parcel of standard Renaissance historiography. Instead, we know them primarily – and indeed can sometimes quote them only – from what their enemies reported they said. The *viri obscuri* – obscurantists to the humanists – have become literally and simply obscure to us. Moreover our post-Enlightenment mentality abhors their use of institutional and statutory conservatism, of inquisition and censorship, and of the inertia of tradition as weapons against our heroes. In this light, however, I suggest that Erasmus' concern in 1527 about the lack of historicism might well be invoked once again today.

For a number of years I have sought to redress one small corner of this imbalance by studying and editing texts emanating from the University of Paris, especially its Faculty of Theology, hoping to throw light on the intellectual, religious, legal, and social environment – in short, the *mentalité* – which produced those texts. In my opinion, nothing less than a series of such researches at the major centres of sixteenth-century institutional and intellectual life will provide the true context of the controversies which the age of Renaissance and Reformation deserves.

At no time have I sought to establish either side as right or wrong. Rather, in examining and explicating a text, I have tried to learn, and to help my reader to learn, how different groups and individuals in sixteenth-century France would have received that text, and how they viewed the University and its controversies with humanists and reformers. In brief, my first charge as an editor and historian has been to situate the text in its own historical context, with no reference to my own opinions or those of the reader.

Of the many different series of charters and registers in Paris archives which provide entry to the Parisian context, I have found the most fruitful to be the magnificent range of manuscript registers kept by the Parlement of Paris and now preserved in the Archives Nationales.[14] The Parlement was a group of about a hundred and twenty French jurists, appointed for life, who constituted several courts of first instance as well as the supreme court of appeals in France. Their registers provide a mirror and a microscope focused on the sixteenth-century French world. Sifting through literally tens of thousands of cases and decisions taken during the thirty-year period from 1520 to 1550, I have come to see that this powerful, influential body of French jurists viewed the ideological struggles of the time in a way quite different from that of Erasmus and his admirers – and from that of most historians who know the controversies through their eyes. It is indeed difficult for us in the twentieth century to grasp the extent of this difference. For example, the jurists regarded blasphemy not merely as bad manners, not only as a sin, but also as a crime against the state – an action susceptible of drawing down the wrath of God upon France.[15] No wonder, then, that they held in greater dread anybody trying to alter the revealed word of God in the Scriptures or anybody they judged as seeking to undermine traditional practices and beliefs of the Church.

Along with the records of the Parlement as a framework, I have used a number of registers kept by the four faculties and the four nations of the University of Paris. The careless scrawl of Simon Le Roux, the University scribe from 1503 to 1535, can often make their consultation discouraging; but they too afford a perspective on the University of Paris and its controversies not even suspected by many historians. They affirm the traditionalists to have constituted a dominant, widespread ideological position in sixteenth-century Paris. From my parallel reading of the Parlement and University texts I conclude that the Faculty of Theology of Paris was the heart of conservatism in France and the Parlement of Paris its right arm. Because of this I have somewhat playfully entitled a recent edition and analysis of texts of University and Parlement documents *Le Parti conservateur au XVIe siècle*.[16] Whether we like it or not, our understanding of the controversies involving humanists and reformers will not be complete without the texts produced by their opponents; and those texts must be read and analysed in their own context, free of the anachronistic sniping that too often impairs our reading of them.

I would like to review now some instances of Erasmus' controversies in Paris where a closer familiarity with the Parisian context can provide some nuance and even correction to common understanding and interpretations of them. From his earliest significant work, the *Antibarbarians*,[17] Erasmus heaped ridicule upon the scholastic method of enquiry[18] and learning which had been the hallmark of Parisian studies since the twelfth century. About one tenth of his *Praise of Folly*[19] consists of gibes aimed at scholastic theologians, who are depicted as supercilious and full of self-importance. In his *Annotations on the New Testament*, in one particularly telling commentary on 1 Timothy 1:6 – St Paul's warning to his disciple against 'vain discussion' – Erasmus supplies a marvellous *copia* of the kind of speculative theological questions he abhors.[20] The *Ratio verae theologiae*[21] accelerates the attack; and from this position the *Colloquies* mount sometimes a brutally direct assault,[22] sometimes a veiled, subtle sapping of the foundations.[23] The result of all this is the caricature of Paris theologians with which we are all familiar.

In contrast, however, to the anti-Erasmian polemic which these attacks opened up early in Flanders, Spain, and Italy, the Paris theologians remained silent for two decades.[24] Clearly they did not rush to judgment; and this judgment may well never have come at all were it not for, first, the arrival on the theological scene of Martin Luther and, second, the rapid spread of texts favourable to him made possible by the recent flourishing of the printing press.

Faced with the reality of Luther, the Paris theologians came to believe that Erasmus' relentless criticism of Church practices and beliefs and his new versions of the Bible gave comfort to Luther and added momentum to his radical critiques. Their concern about printing was not so much the increased number of books as the kinds of readers who had access to them. Matters which in the past would have been debated by professional theologians alone were now opened up to the untrained layman in the public forum – something Erasmus seemed to see as a gain.[25]

The Paris Faculty of Theology was long accustomed to rendering opinions and verdicts on disputed theological and ecclesiastical questions.[26] Moreover the Parlement of Paris considered the Faculty as a kind of 'permanent council in France,' without which the kingdom founded on throne and altar would fall away.[27] The theologians responded to Luther by streamlining their procedures for dealing with heresy.[28] This mechanism was therefore in place, ready to be applied against Erasmus and others as well. The doctors met the threat of the printing press by working in tandem with the Parlement of Paris to censure books.[29] Erasmus was caught in both nets. Time and again Faculty scrutiny and censure of Erasmus was either triggered or abetted by orders from the Parlement for a doctrinal judgment of his books, usually prompted by printers' requests for a 'privilege,' or copyright. This cardinal role of the Parlement of Paris has generally been either neglected or misunderstood by historians, whose knowledge of the Parlement is usually limited to the names of the few judges known to them, and whom they often wrongly presume to have been friendly to the humanist camp.[30]

The polemic with Erasmus took place at two levels: the collective conflict with the Faculty of Theology and the personal exchanges between Erasmus and three Paris theologians, Pierre Cousturier (or Petrus Sutor),[31] Noël Beda, and Josse Clichtove.[32] I shall focus here on the collective, institutional controversy, which is the material I know best. When I refer to the polemic with individuals, I shall sometimes draw on Erika Rummel's book, *Erasmus and his Catholic Critics*,[33] which has helped to fill an enormous gap in Erasmian studies.

Noël Beda, the key figure at both the collective and the personal levels of conflict, had remained aloof from Faculty business for fifteen years after taking his doctorate.[34] But in 1520, realizing that dealing with Luther required a serious marshalling of the Faculty's authority and resources, he proposed reviving the lapsed office of Faculty syndic, and was elected to the position himself. From that time until 1534 Beda orchestrated the actions of the Faculty to oppose all dissent in the Church. His conviction that Erasmus' works were serving the cause of Luther was a catalyst at all stages of the campaign. This same spirit continued to drive Faculty policy for decades after Beda's death in January 1537.

This is not to imply, as Erasmus sometimes did,[35] that Beda and a few henchmen ruled as tyrants over a cowed Faculty.[36] By reading the registers one learns that the approximately one hundred Paris theologians who could be assembled on important business shared Beda's conviction that Erasmus' works weakened the unity of the Church that was deemed particularly expedient during that time of turmoil. The small number of doctors who were sympathetic to Lutheran ideas were either driven from the Faculty or made to recant; the few with Erasmian sympathies found little encouragement. Five of the latter, for example, failed in August 1523 to block a general conclusion that translations and new versions of the Bible, such as those Erasmus proposed 'for the sake of a word,' were doing harm to the Church.[37] The Faculty backed off when King Francis I, who was hoping to attract Erasmus to Paris, forbade publication of the censure; but it authorized Beda to continue examining Erasmus' works on his own.[38]

I have been amazed time and again to see how little weight the king's orders and threats ordinarily carried with the Parlement and even with the University. Just two months after the king's warning, for example, the jurists once again sought the Faculty's opinion of a book of Erasmus, the *Paraphrases on Luke*. The theologians obliged with ten plenary sessions and several committee meetings[39] which produced a verdict censuring the book. The Parlement refused the copyright, and this book never had a separate Paris edition.[40]

Pierre Cousturier, a Paris graduate who had entered the Carthusians in 1511, launched his own attack in 1525. Even before seeing its final version, the Faculty approved Cousturier's book[41] which defended the tradition that St Jerome, aided by divine inspiration, had translated the Bible into the Latin version still used by the Church. Emendations to that text by philologists and 'petty rhetoricians' – the phrase is Cousturier's – were therefore both foolish and blasphemous.[42] Of all his Parisian-trained opponents, Erasmus held Cousturier most in contempt, and invariably descended *ad hominem* in dealing with him.[43] One of the issues between them, as with Beda, was Erasmus' right and competence to publish anything about Scripture and theology.[44] But more about this later.

While this controversy was still in full heat, the Parlement required the Faculty's judgment about several French translations made by the evangelical humanist Louis de Berquin. Two were clearly translations of Erasmus' *Encomium matrimonii* and *Querela pacis*. Two others[45] were of Erasmian texts which Berquin had seasoned with excerpts from Luther and Guillaume Farel – all presented under the name of Erasmus alone.[46] The Faculty's censure fell on all four books.[47] Ten months later, in conjunction with the second trial of Berquin, the theologians again condemned all four books, both under the names of Erasmus as author and of Berquin as translator.[48] During the course of 1527, the Parlement would blatantly ignore and repeatedly defy the king's orders to cease its judicial pursuit of Berquin. The Faculty clearly sided with the Parlement.

Trying to head off Faculty censures, Erasmus had initiated a correspondence with Noël Beda in April 1525. They exchanged eleven letters, and Erasmus addressed others with the same purpose to the Faculty, to the Parlement of Paris, and to King Francis I.[49] Trying conciliation at first, Erasmus asked for Beda's critical comments on his books. Beda replied bluntly that Erasmus was tragically mistaken to think that new Bible versions and translations would promote piety. He pointed to the disturbances in the diocese of Meaux, which he attributed to Lefèvre d'Étaples' biblical translations, and to the Peasants' Revolts in Germany, which he imputed to Luther's vernacular Bible. Erasmus retorted that his programme of joining language studies to theology will make both fields 'resonate Christ'.[50] Don't confuse the Luther tragedy, he warns, with giving the Bible to the people. As with Cousturier, Erasmus reproaches Beda for refusing to address him as a fellow theologian, and charges him with confusing his personal opinions with theology itself.[51] The real innovators, he says, are not the humanists but the scholastics, who have long since replaced the Bible with Aristotle, Averroes, and Duns Scotus.[52] Much as these positions sound convincing to twentieth-century ears, they did not sway the jurists of the Parlement. Upon receiving Erasmus' letter protesting about Beda and the Faculty, the judges simply forwarded it to the Faculty with a request for comments, and sent no response to Erasmus.

Beda's *Annotations*[53] accused Erasmus of casting doubt on Catholic doctrine, and emphasized the great danger for the Church when 'theologizing humanists,' trained in secular disciplines, presume to expound on sacred theology. Replying first with several short pamphlets[54] and a longer tract,[55] Erasmus then played his trump card by telling King Francis I that Beda was ruining the progress and reputation of learning in France and that he was using scare tactics to usurp royal prerogatives.[56] This got immediate results. The king ordered the Parlement to withdraw Beda's *Annotations* from sale. Although the jurists obeyed the king's direct order this time, the registers leave no doubt that the Parlement shared Beda's views.[57] Erasmus himself later admitted that the suppression probably did his own cause more harm than good.[58]

As earlier, both Parlement and Faculty lost little time in getting back to the matter in hand. The omnibus examination most feared by Erasmus actually began in September 1527, once again at the behest of the Parlement.[59] The Faculty set up committees of masters in their separate colleges to study assigned books and to note whatever they found offensive.[60] They voted a special stipend for this project, and set up a precise schedule of three two-hour plenary sessions each week to expedite it.[61] Unfortunately, the registers are mute about these committee meetings, reporting only the final censure two months later.[62]

In 1528, the whole University of Paris took up the censure of Erasmus' *Colloquies*, with the motion that 'under the pretext of eloquence a youth could be more corrupted than instructed by this kind of reading.'[63] All three of the graduate faculties – Theology, Law and Medicine – and two of the four Nations in the Faculty of Arts supported the motion. The other two Nations would have preferred to ask Erasmus to expurgate the *Colloquies* himself;[64] but the rector broke the tie and ordered a general prohibition to be posted immediately on every university bulletin board.[65]

What is especially significant here is that the entire University agreed that the *Colloquies* posed a threat to the faith and morals of young students. And they took this decision despite direct, contrary pressures from Francis I. Right at this time the king, taken in by an anonymous book[66] purporting to list twelve heresies in Beda's book against Erasmus, was seeking a University judgment against Beda. But the University replied that the heresies lay in Erasmus' books, not in Beda's *Annotations*.[67] In fact, whenever a question of religion or theology came before the whole University, it habitually expressed confidence in whatever decision the Faculty of Theology would take. Was this stance the result of a real moral conviction? or was it merely the recognition of the Faculty's statutory rights and monopolies? Probably both; but both were integrally operative in the sixteenth-century context.[68]

After publishing these censures in 1531,[69] the Faculty took no further action against Erasmus until early 1540, when at least three meetings were devoted to censuring both the *Enchiridion militis christiani* and Erasmus' views about the authorship of the Rule of St Augustine.[70] This was also, I suspect, the occasion of the Faculty's only censure of the *Praise of Folly*.[71] The *Colloquies* were reviewed and condemned a second time in 1549, along with six other books sent to the Faculty for examination by the Parlement of Paris.[72]

While finalizing its first printed catalogue of prohibited books in August 1544, the Faculty passed a resolution to include works of Erasmus.[73] This *editio princeps* of all such indexes contained twelve titles of Erasmus;[74] the 1551 edition added two more.[75] By way of comparison, the slightly later Index of the University of Louvain (1546) censured only one single work of Erasmus,[76] whereas the Indexes issued by the Spanish Inquisition between 1551 and 1584 doubled the number condemned by Paris.[77] Those issued by Milan and Venice in 1549 and 1554[78] practically duplicated the list drawn up by Paris.[79]

I close this *cursus* of the Paris controversies with Erasmus by returning to the argument of historicism. In 1548, the Faculty ruled that the errors of Erasmus could not be excused in the same way as those of certain early Fathers whose works antedated official pronouncement on a question. On the contrary, the doctors argued, Erasmus sought to undermine doctrines and interpretations long defined and commonly accepted in the universal Church; and, despite warnings, he persisted in his errors when he ought to have retracted them, as St Augustine had done.[80] Without realizing it, I suspect, and certainly without Erasmus' sense of irony, the Faculty had turned against Erasmus his own words cited here earlier: 'There are many things which it would be the height of impiety to call into question today, while in an earlier age inquiry into those same matters constituted religious fidelity.'

Let us now recall briefly the refusal by Beda and Cousturier to address Erasmus as a theologian. We must, once again, see this matter in its context. In sixteenth-century France, nobility of spirit did not render a commoner a nobleman; prowess in battle did not dub a soldier a knight; nor did fine skill at the workbench make an artisan ipso facto a master in his guild. In the same way, expertise in theology did not make someone a master of theology. The whole order and stability of sixteenth-century society hinged on status, to which one was born, and office, to which one was raised by duly constituted authority. That same social order in France looked first to the professional corps of theologians, the Paris Faculty of Theology – more than to the bishop of Paris or to the pope in Rome – to judge the truth of teachings pertaining to the Christian faith.[81] Even before Beda had written one word against Erasmus he had argued in 1523 that, apart from conviction for heresy, no theologian could be refused his right to take part in such judgments.[82] In this context he and Cousturier were not merely quibbling with Erasmus about not having a recognized degree. They were defending a concept of social order and law fundamental to both Church and State.

A final note on the sticky notion of objectivity. The predilection of historians for humanists and reformers is not surprising, since these latter seemed to open up fresh perspectives on learning and living, while the scholastic doctors seemed to be entangled in the past. Lucien Febvre epitomized this idealization of humanists and reformers when he described them as 'the very best, the most generous, the most alive' in their age.[83] Whether one agrees or disagrees with Febvre, I maintain that the expression of that kind of judgment is a luxury which editors of texts should be slow to indulge.[84]

One reader of my 1990 edition gently chided me for failing to draw my readers' attention to perceived dangers to reform, progress, and enlightenment posed by Faculty opposition to Bible translations. Such criticism, I think, contains a kind of Whiggish reading of the texts, ignoring the fact that in early sixteenth-century French society most established authorities and powers believed that altering the text of the Bible threatened good order and put in danger the salvation of souls. Editors and historians who disregard that context do so at their own peril and at the peril of their readers.

I turn now from this issue to some concrete problems and decisions in my editorial experience of the Paris texts. Of the three volumes of texts that I have published, two contain the proceedings or conclusions of 846 meetings of the Paris Faculty of Theology from 1524 to 1550.[85] A third, slim volume contains documents of the Parlement and the University reacting to certain key issues of humanism and reform.[86] Since all three are diplomatic editions, I made the conscious decision to reproduce the original orthography and syntax of the registers, leaving all the inconsistencies, solecisms, and gallicisms that so irritated the humanists. In fact, the Latin usage of the Faculty scribes shows that the scholastics and the humanists of the period literally did not speak the same language. I have, of course, emended misspellings and grammatical errors, signalling these and scribal changes in a critical apparatus placed not at the bottom of each page but at the end of the text for each session.

In my opinion, the historical annotations in a diplomatic edition are more valuable than the critical apparatus. I have been fortunate in getting publishers to cooperate in placing the historical notes squarely at the bottom of each page where they can best serve the reader. But here is where I must be especially careful. My attempt to clarify the text, to frame it in its full historical context, must never interfere with the reader's right to confront it free of any interpretation of it I may have formed.

The two Faculty registers I have edited are sequential, the second beginning in November 1533 where the first leaves off. But the two have some startling differences. Because the first register dropped out of sight in December 1533, and came to light only in 1898, its text and margins are completely free of later scribal changes or notations. The second register, however, remained in the Faculty archives, where it served as a reference book for later bedels and historians. As a result it contains numerous marginalia, underlinings, and corrections. For reasons of clarity and esthetics (and to give due prominence to the original text) I relegate all such matters to the critical apparatus, leaving in the margin an alphabetical signal enclosed in square brackets.

Editing the second register posed a major problem. In its last section beginning in October 1546 and stretching to March 1, 1550, it betrays a serious degeneration in both the internal quality of the minutes and their external, physical presentation. Trying to understand the reason for this, I considered but rejected the idea that the Faculty, whether for reasons of the bedel's absence, health, or neglect, simply failed to maintain its earlier high reporting standards. I have concluded instead that the fascicles containing the proceedings for 1546–1557 had been lost, and that in the latter year two different scribes attempted to reconstitute the record for 1546 to 1550. Consulting the *plumitifs* (sketchy notes taken at the meetings intended as an aid to the bedel's redaction of the proceedings), they did the best they could to report on the meetings that had taken place a decade earlier. It is obvious, though, that the two scribes did not work together in this project, since they sometimes produced two different records from the same *plumitif*, and even, in four cases, assigned them different year dates. This posed the editorial decision of choosing one version over the other and of using the critical and the historical apparatus to point out significant variations in the two accounts. The one advantage of this thorny problem was that it gave me a real appreciation of the method and process the bedels normally used in drawing up their reports.

Since indexes are an essential tool to give access to an edited text, I believe it important to devote all the time and space required to make them as complete as possible. I generally sub-divide any entry that consists of more than five page references. For my most recent volume I compiled three indexes extending over 77 pages, or 154 columns, i.e. nearly one column for every three pages of text and notes. This kind of indexing is grueling work but is never thankless. Readers will never cease to sing the praises of the editor who produces a careful index or set of indexes.

In closing, it grieves me to report that, were I starting my research and editorial work in Paris in 1994 instead of 1971, it would no longer be possible for me to accomplish what I was able to do in the past. Officials at the Archives Nationales in Paris are increasingly reluctant to grant researchers access to original charters and registers. While their concern about the physical condition of the originals is sometimes warranted, quite often those documents, written on parchment and bound in leather, are more durable than many books produced today. The archivists argue – correctly, up to a point – that a good microfilm permits accurate and adequate consultation of the page. This assumes, of course, that the microfilm is good and that no pages have been inadvertently skipped by the photographer – a situation which all too often occurs. It also assumes that folio numbers (often added in pencil) are legible, which is often not the case. Further, even excellent microfilm readers make physically exhausting and prohibitively time-consuming the kind of rapid searching through vast quantities of materials which has yielded me a rich harvest of findings. This misery is compounded at the Archives Nationales by the equipment now in use: because the glass plates designed to hold the film in focus proved to scratch the films, the officials have simply removed those plates, with the result that the machines will no longer hold their focus. As a result of these policies and conditions, all the physical advantages of the codex have been retrogressivly set aside, forcing a reversion to the ancient process of unrolling the scroll. A meeting held on 6 April 1994 between about twenty-five researchers in Paris and officials of the Archives to discuss these problems adjourned without success. While the archive officials are willing to grant access to original documents when they are to be published, the current policy makes it difficult to discover the texts that merit publishing. Equally serious, the essential process that I have advocated above – establishing the historical context for new editions of texts – will be more difficult in future than it has been in the past.

NOTES

1 P.S. Allen, ed, *Opus epistolarum Desiderii Erasmi Roterodami*, 11 vols and index (Oxford 1906–58), Ep 1544; cf. *Collected Works of Erasmus* (Toronto 1974–) Ep 1544, trans Charles Fantazzi, ed J.K. Farge (forthcoming). Erasmus' edition of Origen was published as the *Fragmentum commentariorum Origenis in Euangelium secundum Matthaeum* (Basel: Froben 1527).

2 *Opera omnia Desiderii Erasmi Roterodami* (Amsterdam 1969–) I–3 531–2, lines 1318–78. For the English translation, see *The Colloquies of Erasmus*, trans and ed Craig R. Thompson (Chicago 1965) 351–3. Craig Thompson's new, extensively annotated edition will constitute vols. 39–40 of the CWE.

3 See J.K. Farge, *Biographical Register of Paris Doctors of Theology, 1500–1536* (Toronto 1980) 31-36, no 34.

4 Erasmus does, in one line, cover his tracks in this regard, saying 'Perhaps these conditions have been corrected; but too late, obviously, for those who have died or who carry a diseased body about.' See *The Colloquies of Erasmus* (Chicago 1965) 353; cf ASD I–3 532:1368–9.

5 The philanthropy came from private and royal patrons, including Kings Louis XII and Francis I. See Marcel Godet, *La Congrégation de Montaigu* (Paris 1912) 184–6; and *Catalogue des actes de François Ier* 5: 541, no 17452.

6 G. Codina Mir, S.J., *Aux sources de la pédagogie des Jésuites* (Rome 1968) 69.

7 Marcel Godet, *La Congrégation de Montaigu*, 186–9.

8 Montaigu became the first Paris college to establish classes, or levels

of instruction. See G. Codina Mir, S.J., *Aux sources de la pédagogie des Jésuites*, 101, 102.

9 More arts graduates of the Collège de Montaigu took doctorates in theology than those of any other arts college. See J.K. Farge, *Orthodoxy and Reform in Early Reformation France* (Leiden 1985), 72–3.

10 Among them John Mair, Jacques Almain, David Cranston, Robert Caubraith, William Manderston, António and Luis Coronel, Gaspar Lax, and Robert Céneau.

11 See his oft-quoted passage on the Collège de Montaigu: 'si j'estois roy de Paris, le diable m'emport si je ne metoys le feu dedans et faisoys brusler et principal et regens qui endurent ceste inhumanité davant leurs yeulx estre exercée!' (*Gargantua*, ch XXXVII). In the *Quart livre*, ch 21, Rabelais calls Beda's successor Pierre Tempête a 'grand fouet- teur d'escholiers.'

12 The late Walter S. Bense, Jr., whose 1967 dissertation is the most careful study of Beda ever undertaken, decried the persistent histori- cal bias against Beda in these terms: 'For a generation that ought to have learned to appreciate the value of intelligent opposition and "resistance" to political absolutism and the exaggerated claims of new ideologies – however much these may cloak themselves in the mantle of some past golden age – Beda may perhaps hope for a revision of the judgment passed on him by his enemies and all too easily perpe- tuated in the Ages of Absolutism and Liberalism which followed the Humanist Reformtion' (*Noël Beda and the Humanist Reformation at Paris, 1504–1534* [Harvard University PhD dissertation 1967], Introduction xvi).

13 They are not entirely lacking, of course. One notable example is the series 'Corpus Catholicorum' which, over the last seventy-five years, has produced almost fifty volumes of German Catholic controversy of the Reformation.

14 Over the course of several years, I have examined every page of the primary series known as the *Registres du Conseil* for the years 1520 to 1550, and have searched in particular cases through the parallel registers of pleas (the *Plaidoiries*, both the *Matinées* and the *Après-dinées* series). My research in the equally fascinating registers of the *cours criminel* has been on a more limited, ad hoc basis.

15 J.K. Farge, *Le parti conservateur au XVIe siècle: Université et Parlement de Paris à l'époque de la Renaissance et de la Réforme*, Textes et inédits du Collège de France (Paris 1992) 59–66.

16 See the preceding note.

17 Although not published until 1520, this work was based solidly on notebooks composed as early as 1488; see CWE 23, trans and ed Margaret Mann Phillips (Toronto 1978) ix; cf ASD I-1 1–138, ed Kazimierz Kumaniecki.

18 For example, Erasmus' burgomaster says: 'When languages were neglected and antiquity was neglected too, there grew up a confused sort of teaching, a kind of uneducated erudition, which corrupted not only humane studies but, in distressing ways, theology itself' (CWE 23, 26).

19 CWE 27, 78–153; ASD IV-3, 72–194

20 Cited by Craig R. Thompson, 'Better teachers than Scotus or Aquinas,' *Medieval and Renaissance Studies*, ed John L. Lievsay, series 2 (Durham, NC 1968) 141–5 note 58. We are likewise fortunate to have Erika Rummel's recent study of the *Annotations*, which puts into high relief Erasmus' quarrels with traditional theology and exegesis. See *Erasmus' Annotations on the New Testament: From Philologist to Theologian* (Toronto 1986).

21 *Desiderii Erasmi Roterodami Opera omnia* ed J. Leclerc (Leiden 1703–6; repr 1961–2) v, 76–138

22 As in 'A Fish Diet' and 'The Meeting of the Philological Society.' For the *Colloquies* see note 2.

23 In 'The Godly Feast' the host and his guests – all laymen, none trained in theology – expound the Pauline themes of grace and freedom in the light of classical authors. They proclaim the power of secular poetry to be more edifying, even in moral questions, than all the teachings of the scholastics. See Craig R. Thompson, 'Better Teachers than Scotus or Aquinas,' 114–37; idem *The Colloquies of Erasmus* (Chicago 1965) 46–78.

24 The sole exception was their attack on Jean Briselot, a Paris graduate of 1500 who rose to become confessor to the future Charles V; but these attacks occurred in Brabant. See Allen Epp 597, 608, 628, 641, 695, 739, 794; cf the corresponding English versions in CWE 5.

25 Erasmus welcomed and catered to this new readership. The theologians took special exception to his promotion of vernacular Bibles which would be 'read by the uneducated, ... even the lowliest women,' by Scots and Irish, Turks and Saracens. See his *Paraclesis, id est Adhortatio ad christianae philosophiae studium* LB 5 138–43; English translation by John C. Olin in *Christian Humanism and the Reformation: Selected Writings of Erasmus* 3rd ed (New York 1987) 97–108, especially 101.

26 See J.K. Farge, *Orthodoxy and Reform*, 115.

27 J.K. Farge, *Le parti conservateur*, 69–73

28 See J.K. Farge, *Orthodoxy and Reform* 41–2, 127. The Faculty also increased the frequency and the length of their meetings (ibid 37).

29 See J.K. Farge, 'Introduction historique' in J.-M. De Bujanda, F. M. Higman, and J.K. Farge, *Index de l'Université de Paris, 1544, 1545, 1547, 1549, 1551, 1556*, Vol. 1 of *Index des livres interdits*, ed J.-M. De Bujanda (Sherbrooke 1985). See also J.K. Farge, 'Early Censorship in Paris: A New Look at the Roles of the Parlement of Paris and of King Francis I,' *Renaissance and Reformation/Renaissance et Réforme* 25/2 (1989) 173–83.

30 They point correctly to two friends of Guillaume Budé, François Deloynes and Louis Ruzé, but the one died in 1524 and the other left the Parlement about that same time. Budé himself came only rarely to sessions of the Parlement. But they also assume, and wrongly, that Jean de Selve, the *premier président* of the Parlement until his death in August 1529, was a friend of Erasmus, because Erasmus dedicated a book to him. On the contrary, Selve was completely traditionalist, as were his associate presidents Charles Guillard and Antoine Le Viste and his successor Pierre Lizet.

31 J.K. Farge, *Biographical Register of Paris Doctors of Theology* 119–21, no 123

32 Ibid 90–104, no 101

33 2 vols (Nieuwkoop 1989)

34 Apart from his direction of the Collège de Montaigu (until 1514), Beda had been concerned with moralistic and disciplinary issues like gambling and the qualifications for holding benefices. He criticized certain humanistic exegetical issues raised by Jacques Lefèvre d'Étaples and Josse Clichtove, such as the plurality of Marys in the New Testament. He also took a major role in the University of Paris' fight against King Francis I's Concordat with Pope Leo X.

35 In Ep 1721 to the Parlement of Paris, Ep 1722 to King Francis I, and Ep 1723 to the Faculty of Theology, for example, Erasmus repeatedly lays the blame for his persecution on Beda, Cousturier, and others of their ilk, avoiding criticism of the Faculty in general.

36 In fact, Beda tried to resign at least three times (in 1522, 1524, and 1527), but each time the Faculty prevailed upon him to continue in office (*Orthodoxy and Reform*, 42).

37 'Deinde auditis omnibus conclusit sacra Facultas organo domini decani Boussart, quod non sunt utiles Ecclesie nove traductiones

biblie, que de greco vel hebreo in latinum fiunt, verbi causa per Erasmum et Jacobum Fabrum, sed pernitiose ... et ideo nullomodo permittende aut tollerande sed per Ecclesie prelatos omni via ab Ecclesia elim[in]ande.' See J.-A. Clerval, ed, *Registre des procès-verbaux de la Faculté de théologie de l'Université de Paris*, 1 (1505–1523), (Paris 1917) 379–80; cf the antecedents to this: 356, 357, 377.

38 Ibid 401–2

39 See James K. Farge, ed, *Registre des procès-verbaux de la Faculté de Théologie de l'Université de Paris* 1-2 (1524–1533), (Paris 1990), nos 4B, 5A, 6B, 7E, 8A, 9A, 10A, 11A, 16A, 18C; the meetings stretched from January to April 1524.

40 Pierre Regnault included this Paraphrase in his omnibus edition of the *Paraphrases* (Paris 1540). This may have helped spark the renewal of Faculty investigation of Erasmus at that time.

41 *De tralatione Bibliae* (Pierre Vidoue for Jean Petit: 28 February 1525 n.st.); see B. Moreau, *Inventaire chronologique des éditions parisiennes* 3 (Abbeville 1985) 247, no 803. For the Faculty's approval, see *Procès-verbaux* 1-2 61, no 53F (1 October 1524).

42 Replying to specific points, Cousturier relied somewhat on earlier critics of Erasmus like Edward Lee and Diego de Zúñiga – but especially on notes sent to him by Noël Beda.

43 *Apologia adversus debacchationes Petri Sutoris* (Basel: Johann Froben 1525).

44 Complaining of Cousturier's refusal to acknowledge him as a fellow theologian, Erasmus claimed '[I have] more than once rejected the title [of theologian] tendered to me by celebrated universities, and I finally accepted it with some misgivings from a university that is not without renown.' (I cite Erika Rummel's translation of LB 745C, in *Erasmus and his Catholic Critics* 2, 68.) Cousturier retorted in his *Antapologia adversus insanam Erasmi apologiam* (Paris: Pierre Vidoue for Jean Petit, February 1526), mocking Erasmus' status as 'a new type of professor ... from a university that is "not without renown" but which he does not name and which is unknown to me – and a hapless university it is for granting a degree to such an antitheologian (if it did grant it)' (trans E. Rummel, *Erasmus and his Catholic Critics* 2, 68). Erasmus and Cousturier continued their polemic in later pamphlets and in correspondence with third parties.

45 The titles are *Brevis admonitio de modo orandi* and *Symbolum* (the colloquy *Inquisitio de fide*). See *Procès-verbaux* 1–2 96, no 94A.

46 See Margaret Mann [Phillips], 'Louis de Berquin, traducteur d'Erasme,' *Revue du seizième siècle* 18 (1931) 309–23.

47 The *Querela pacis* was condemned to be burned: see ibid. nos 94A, 95A and notes 1525:44 and 46. Josse Clichtove, having already renounced some of his earlier humanistic conclusions, undertook to refute Erasmus' *Encomium matrimonii* in his *Propugnaculum ecclesiae adversus Lutheranos* (Paris: Simon de Colines 1526).

48 This formal condemnation came at this time as part of the case against Berquin, whom the Parlement had arrested for the second time.

49 I have analyzed this correspondence at greater length in my *Orthodoxy and Reform in Early Reformation France* 187–93. See likewise Erika Rummel, *Erasmus and his Catholic Critics* 2, 30–3.

50 Allen Ep 1581:115

51 Allen Ep 1679

52 Allen Ep 1679:31–5

53 (Paris: Josse Bade 1526; Cologne: Pierre Quentell 1527). The book also purported to refute the exegetical work of Jacques Lefèvre d'Étaples. The Faculty gave its approval on 26 May 1526 (*Procès-verbaux*, 1–2 137, no 152B). For further analysis of this, see Erika Rummel, *Erasmus and his Catholic Critics* 2, 33–43.

54 *Prologus supputationis errorum in censuris Beddae* (LB 9 442–51), *Divinationes ad notata per Beddam de Paraphrasi Erasmi* (LB 9 453–96), *Elenchus in Natalis Beddae censuras erroneas* (LB 9 496–514), and the *Responsio ad notulas Beddaicis* (LB 9 702–20)

55 *Supputatio calumniarum Natalis Bedae* (Basel: Froben March 1527); LB 9, 516–702; cf Erika Rummel, *Erasmus and his Catholic Critics* 2, 38.

56 Allen Ep 1722 (16 June 1526)

57 Paris Archives nationales X^{1A} 1529 f 367v–9v (17 August 1526); *Procès-verbaux* 1–2, 142–3 no. 161B-C; cf J.K. Farge, *Orthodoxy and Reform* 260–1. Nothing confirms the report of Levinus Ammonius about a humiliating order forcing Beda himself to notify each Paris bookseller about the suppression of his book (Allen Ep 1763:46–58).

58 Allen Ep 2188:211–12

59 *Procès-verbaux*, 1–2, 160 182B (10 December 1526). One correspondent told Erasmus that the *Colloquies*, the *Praise of Folly* and the *Parabolae* were all condemned (Allen Ep 1784:5–8 [Nicolaus Vesuvius to Erasmus, 8 February 1527]). Vesuvius, however, did not reside in Paris and admits his news is second-hand. While the *Colloquies* had indeed been examined and censured in May 1526 (*Procès-verbaux* 1–2, 149A, 149E, 151B, 152A), no record exists of a Paris censure of the *Folly* before 1540 or of the *Parabolae* at all. The earliest evidence of a censure of the *Praise of Folly* is reported in the hand of Philippe Bouvot, a

seventeenth-century bedel of the Faculty of Theology, who added the title as number 65 to his own earlier list of 64 books condemned by the Faculty and sent to the Parlement of Paris in April 1543 (Paris AN Reg MM 248 f 181r–v; cf J.K. Farge, *Registre des conclusions de la Faculté de l'Université de Paris*, du 26 Novembre 1533 au 1er mars 1550 (Paris 1994) Appendix 3, 453–60. For Faculty deliberation on this, see ibid. 259D, 260A, 261A, 262A [1, 2, 10 March, 14 April 1543]). Although these deliberations do not specifically mention Erasmus, the list does include the *Enchiridion* as number 21. D'Argentré, *Collectio judiciorum de novis erroribus*, 2–1, 234–6, misreads Bouvot's '27^a jan[ua]^{rii} 1540', reading instead '27^a junii 1542', and the *Index de l'Université de Paris* (Sherbrooke 1985) 444 copied this erroneous reading. In his edition of the Faculty's censures of the *Moria*, d'Argentré (2–1, 229–32) dates them – erroneously again, I maintain – 27 January 1542 (old style). Since the Faculty's conclusions record no attention to Erasmus at that time, I believe these censures reflect instead the conclusions reached about Erasmus in January 1540 (see note 70 below). However, Bouvot, who compiled his records several decades after adoption of the new style of dating, usually copied dates prior to Easter as he found them, i.e. in the old style. If, then, his '1540' really means '1541,' new style, the resulting date of 27 January 1541 would not enjoy the same corroborating evidence from the Faculty proceedings as does the date 27 January 1540. With respect to the *Parabolae siue similia*, an expurgated edition was published in 1529 by Claude Berthot, a theology student who became a doctor of theology in 1542.

60 *Procès-verbaux* 1–2, 179 no 212B

61 Ibid 180–1, 214A (12 October 1526)

62 16 December 1527. Far from comprehensive, however, it censures only the *Paraphrases*, the *Annotations* on the New Testament, the rebuttals of Beda, the *De esu carnium*, and the Preface to his edition of St Hilary. In many respects this collective censure merely took up Beda's private polemic which had been thwarted by the king's seizure of Beda's book.

63 *Procès-verbaux* 1–2, 137 152A (16 May 1526)

64 They would have preferred to ask Erasmus to suppress the offending passages voluntarily.

65 See d'Argentré, *Collectio judiciorum* 2–1, 52.

66 *Duodecim articuli infidelitatis Bedae* (Paris: [Josse Bade] 1527). Often attributed to Louis de Berquin, the book is more likely the work of Jacques Merlin, whose defence of the church Father Origen had been denounced by Beda.

67 See Archives de l'Université de Paris (Bibliothèque de la Sorbonne),
    Registre 16 ('Registrum congregationum conclusionum ordinum
    universitatis et deputatorum eiusdem') f 87r, 87v, 88r, 88v.

68 In the 1530s and 1540s, the French monarchy would become increas-
    ingly concerned about the inroads of heresy, and often assisted the
    Faculty and even prodded the Parlement to suppress the Reformation.
    In 1535, Francis I issued the most draconion edict of censorship ever
    seen (*Ordonnances des rois de France: Règne de François Ier* [Paris, 1902–]
    7 203–4; see also J.K. Farge, 'Early Censorship in Paris: A New Look
    at the Roles of the Parlement of Paris and of King Francis I,' *Renais-
    sance and Reformation/Renaissance et Réforme* XXV 2 [1989] 173–83). He
    welcomed the Faculty's twenty-six Articles of Faith in 1543, and his
    son Henry II authorized the censure of the humanist printer Robert
    Estienne – a serious blow to the cause of humanism and reform in
    France. Such developments tell us about the increasing strength of
    traditionalist attitudes of the age and about the brute facts of its
    politics. Clearly, given this context, the accusations launched against
    the Paris theologians as lacking political sense and even common
    sense require some revision.

69 *Determinatio facultatis super quamplurimis assertionibus Desiderii Erasmi
    Roterodami* (Paris: Josse Bade 1531; 2nd ed: n.d. but after July 1531).
    See Ph. Renouard, *Imprimeurs et libraires parisiens du XVIe siècle* 2 (Paris
    1967) no 774.

70 Paris, AN Reg MM 248, f 59r–v, 60r (15, 31 January, 5 February 1540;
    cf J.K. Farge, *Registre des conclusions*, nos 187A, 187E, 187F, 189A). The
    doctors likewise approved Richard Du Mans' *Antidotum contra Erasmi
    censuram in regulam divi Augustini*, which appeared in the *Opera* of
    Augustine (Paris: Yolande Bonhomme and Charlotte Guillard 1541).
    D'Argentré, *Collectio judiciorum*, records five different censures of the
    Enchiridion, four by the Faculty and one by the Parlement of Paris.
    The first (1–2, Index X) is homologous to our entry from AN Reg MM
    248 cited above in this note. The second (2–1, 133–4 [14 February 1544
    n.st.]) records the Parlement's censures of the French translation, *Le
    chevalier chrétien*, and of *La manière de se confesser* (a translation of the
    Exomologesis). The third (2–1, 135 [2 March 1543 n st]) censures both
    the Latin original and the French translation published by Étienne
    Dolet, and is number 21 on the manuscript list of 65 censured books
    sent to the Parlement (see above, note 54). The fourth (2–1, 227 [1
    September 1543]) reveals the censure of the Latin *Enchiridion* among a
    group of books sent to the Faculty by the Parlement. The fifth (2–1,
    229–32 [27 January 1543 n.st.]) records a censure of the *Enchiridion*

(called here the *Confessio militis christiani*) together with several of the *Colloquies* and a lengthy censure of the *Moriae encomium*. Only the first of the five can be documented in the register of *Conclusions* of Faculty meetings (AN MM 248). However, because d'Argentré already misdated a censure of 27 January 1540 (n.st.) for 27 June 1542, I am inclined to identify the last of the five with the Faculty censures issuing from the deliberations of early 1540 (see note 59 above).

71 The sources, none original, place this censure variously in January 1540 (n.st.), June 1542, and January 1543 (n.st.); see above, notes 59 and 70. Unfortunately, the manuscript register of Faculty doctrinal determinations after 1540 is not extant.

72 J.K. Farge, *Registre des conclusions* 412, no 427A

73 Paris AN Reg MM 248 f 103; cf J.K. Farge *Registre des conclusions* 278, no 303A.

74 *Modus orandi Deum* (1523); *Exomologesis sive modus confitendi* (1524); *Enchiridion militis christiani* (1503); *De interdicto esu carnium* (1522); *Encomium moriae, cum commentario* (1511); *Colloquia* (1518, etc.); *Paraphrases in Novum Testamentum* (1517–24, 1534; complete Paris ed 1540); the *Scholia* on the works of St Jerome (1516); the *Prologue* to the works of St Hilary (1523); *Christiani matrimonii institutio* (1526); the *Censura in regulam divi Augustini* (1529); and the *Liber de sarcienda ecclesiae concordia* (1533). See J.-M. de Bujanda, F.M. Higman and J.K. Farge, *Index de l'Université de Paris*, vol 1 of the series Index des livres interdits (Sherbrooke 1985) 176–81.

75 *Annotationes in Novum Testamentum* (1516, etc.) and *Ecclesiastes sive de ratione concionandi* (1535). See *Index de l'Université de Paris* 178, 181.

76 The *Liber de sarcienda ecclesiae concordia*: see J.-M. De Bujanda, *Index de l'Université de Louvain*, vol 2, Index des livres interdits (Sherbrooke 1986) 307.

77 J.-M. De Bujanda, *Index de l'Inquisition espagnole 1551, 1554, 1559* and *Index de l'Inquisition espagnole 1583, 1584*, vols 5 and 6 of Index des livres interdits; (Sherbrooke 1984, 1993)

78 J.-M. De Bujanda, *Index de Venise (1549), Venise et Milan (1554)* Index des livres interdits 3 (Sherbrooke 1987) 265–268

79 De Bujanda surveys the censure of Erasmus in the sixteenth century, in 'Erasme dans les index des livres interdits,' in *Langage et vérité. Etudes offertes à Jean-Claude Margolin* ed Jean Céard (Geneva 1993) 31–47.

80 From a document copied by Philippe Bouvot in the seventeenth century, dated 1548; see Bibliothèque S.-Sulpice, MS 27, f 199v–200v; see also *Collectio quorumdam gravium authorum, qui ex professo, vel ex*

occasione sacrae Scripturae, aut diuinorum officiorum, in vulgarem linguam Translationes, damnarunt. Vna cvm decretis summi pontificis, & cleri Gallicani, eiusque Epistolis, Sorbonae Censuris, ac supremi Parisiensis Senatus placitis. Iussu ac mandato eiusdem Cleri Gallicani edita (Paris: Antoine Vitré 1661) 14–16. This latter work was probably occasioned by the renewal of the condemnation at that time of Erasmus' *Colloquies*: see J.K. Farge, *Registre des conclusions* 412, no 427A.

81 D'Argentré, *Collectio judiciorum* 1–2, 411. See J.K. Farge, *Orthodoxy and Reform* 115, 160–2.

82 'Documentum, quo docetur nullum theologum debere arceri ab examine doctrinarum Fidei, nisi fuerit suspectus in fide,' written in 1522 to refute Jacques Merlin. See d'Argentré, *Collectio judiciorum de novis erroribus* 1–2, 410–12.

83 Lucien Febvre, 'Une question mal posée: Les origines de la réforme française et le problème des causes de la Réforme,' *Revue historique* CLXI (1929); repr *Au coeur religieux du XVIe siècle*, 2d ed (Paris 1968) 69; English translation by K. Folca, 'The Origins of the French Reformation: a badly-put question?,' in *A New Kind of History* ed Peter Burke (New York and London 1973) 44–107.

84 I do not, of course, deny the inevitability or desirability of finding meaning for the present in an historical text. But this should be a second reflex, following upon the prior examination of the text in the context of its own time and milieu.

85 See above, notes 39 and 59.

86 See above, note 15.

2 Editing Genevan Ecclesiastical Registers

More than forty years ago, when I was a graduate student working on my doctoral dissertation in Geneva, I received a letter from Roland Bainton, probably the most prominent specialist on Reformation history at that time. He was finishing his biography of Servetus, and had just discovered that during the Servetus trial John Calvin had been delivering a series of sermons on the Old Testament book of Ezekiel and that these sermons had never been published. He asked me to look at these sermons to see if they contained any references or allusions to the Servetus trial. I went to the Musée historique de la Réformation in the Geneva University Library where these materials were then kept. I was brought two enormous volumes containing manuscript transcripts of these sermons, copied down as Calvin preached them by a secretary hired by the city government. I had nearly finished my year of research in Geneva and was about to return to the United States. I had to report to Bainton that there was simply no way I could read through all these sermons in the time remaining to me. He proceeded to publish his biography of Servetus without exploring this avenue of possible research. These sermons remain unpublished, along with a good many others Calvin preached during his ministry in Geneva. Before the Second World War, Hanns Rückert began the work of editing these unpublished sermons and the Neu-kirchener Verlag in 1936 published his edition of Calvin's sermons on 2 Samuel as the first in a projected series titled the *Supplementa Calviniana*. That project was interrupted by the war but was revived afterwards under the auspices of the World Alliance of Reformed Churches. Sets of sermons were assigned to individual editors. This project is still proceeding, but slowly. Several of the original editors have died, including those asked to edit the Ezekiel sermons. New editors have had to be named. It will be some time before we see all this material in print. To this day I do not know whether Calvin ever mentioned or alluded to Servetus and his doctrines in the course of his sermons on Ezekiel. Neither, to my knowledge, does anyone else.

I tell this story to illustrate an important fact about the current state of Calvin studies. There have been and are dozens of scholars special-izing on John Calvin and his thought. There is an International Con-gress on Calvin Research that meets every four years, most recently in Edinburgh in September of 1994. There is a Calvin Studies Society for North Americans that meets every other year in 1995 in Grand Rapids. There is a group of American scholars in the southern part of the United States that meets periodically to discuss Calvin studies. But many of these scholars seem to be only dimly aware of the fact that many of the raw materials needed for research in this field are not as yet available. They depend for their work on the fifty-nine volumes of the *Calvini Opera* published between 1863 and 1900. Many of them, indeed, limit themselves to examination of a single great book, Calvin's *Institutes of the Christian Religion,* and devote their energies to re-examining it and evaluating its utility for modern Christians. I do not want to deprecate all of this scholarly energy. But I do want to plead for more attention to the source materials by and about Calvin that remain unavailable. I want to plead for more work to make them avail-able. Calvin, it seems to me, is a figure of sufficient importance to western history to deserve study based on all of the relevant sources by a spectrum of scholars going well beyond those who claim to be his spiritual descendants.

Of these sources, the ones that happen to interest me most are the registers of ecclesiastical bodies in which Calvin was active. They include the registers of the Company of Pastors over which Calvin presided as Moderator, from his recall to Geneva from Strasbourg in 1541 until his death in 1564. They also include the registers of the Consistory, which he insisted that Geneva establish to control the behaviour of everyone in the community. It was duly established in 1541, as a part of the bargain that brought him back to Geneva, and he remained active in it until his death. Both of these bodies met once a week. Each selected a secretary to keep records of its meetings. The early secretaries of the Company of Pastors were themselves pastors and kept rather desultory records. They wrote down decisions of its weekly meetings only occasionally. They also inserted into these registers extended reports of special activities in which the Company got involved. The early secretaries of the Consistory were professional notaries who were paid for their work in keeping these records and who were much more conscientious. They kept weekly minutes of each meeting and most of them survive, with only a few lacunae. All of these registers remain the property of the Eglise Nationale Protestante de Genève, which is incidentally still governed in part by a Company of Pastors and a Consistory. These registers have been placed on deposit in the Geneva State Archives and are there available for consultation by scholars. In addition microfilm copies of these registers have been made, along with a number of other Genevan manuscript materials of relevance. Copies of them can be found on deposit in several American libraries. The largest sets of which I have knowledge are to be found in the Meeter Center for Calvin Studies at the Calvin College and Seminary in Grand Rapids, Michigan.

The existence of these registers has long been known and they have, in fact, been consulted by scholars. The *Calvini Opera* in the *Corpus Reformatorum* (Brunswick 1863–1900), for example, contains in its twenty-first volume an 'Annales Calviniani,' a day-by-day chronology of Calvin's career based on extracts from these registers, correspondence, and other records. In addition back in the nineteenth century a selection of extracts from the Consistory registers was transcribed by a local scholar named Frédéric-Auguste Cramer and distributed in 1853 in a number of sets made through a primitive method of photocopying.[1] But both these collections and other uses of these registers are flawed, often seriously.

I discovered this more than forty years ago when I went to Geneva as a graduate student. I had decided to prepare a doctoral dissertation based on a prosopography of all the pastors sent from Geneva to France between 1555 and 1562, the critical years leading up to the French wars of religion. Many of these 'missionaries' had been commissioned by the Geneva Company of Pastors and their names were recorded in its registers. A nineteenth-century Genevan scholar named Gaberel had published a list of their names. That was the starting point for my dissertation. The day I arrived in the Geneva State Archives I called up my first volume of registers and discovered to my horror that I could not read it. I found out that any European scholar who wishes to work on a subject of this kind must first master a discipline known as paleography. Ideally he (or she) would go to an institution like the Ecole des Chartes in Paris that specializes in teaching paleography. A Genevan specialist on the period of the Reformation named Paul-F. Geisendorf, later to be named Professor of National History at the University of Geneva, was then teaching a regular course in paleography, and I asked him if I could take it. He told me not to bother. He was in the archives every day and he could help me when I got stuck. For the next three months, M. Geisendorf and M. Vaucher, the director of the Archives, gave me what amounted to an intensive personal course in paleography. In the end I could read those registers myself.

When I then re-examined the registers of the Geneva Company of Pastors, I discovered that M. Gaberel was not a good paleographer. He had made some serious errors in the list that I had been using as my starting point. He had, for example, read one name in three different ways. These mistaken readings had been picked up by local historians in several parts of France. That meant that the bibliography of local studies I had painstakingly compiled before coming to Geneva contained repeated references to two men on his list of 'missionary' pastors who had in fact never existed. They were simply paleographic errors. Gaberel's list also contained other references to other pastors who had never been further identified. They had never been fully identified because their names had never been correctly read.

This experience drove home for me the fundamental importance of paleography for any serious study of European manuscripts of this period. It also helps explain, I am convinced, why so few of the many scholars specializing on Calvin attempt to use the unpublished sources on his thought and career. Most serious Calvin specialists study him from his Latin writings. They are much less likely to study him in French. They are not equipped to study him in French manuscript.

Several years later, I got my first opportunity to edit those registers. A wealthy American philanthropist who wished to remain anonymous sent a representative to Geneva to offer to do something for Calvin studies. It was this representative who arranged for all those microfilms now available in Grand Rapids and elsewhere. He also wanted to arrange for publication of the most important of these materials. I happened to be in Geneva on research leave that year. My mentors in the Archives referred this American representative to me, and I proposed an edition of the registers of the Company of Pastors for the period of Calvin's ministry. I enlisted the help of two Swiss friends, who were both graduates of the Ecole des Chartes, and thus accomplished paleographers. They were Jean-François Bergier, now a distinguished economic historian at the Swiss Federal Institute of Technology in Zurich, and Alain Dufour until recently the managing director of the Librairie Droz in Geneva. I prepared an annotated transcription of the better part of the second volume of these registers, the section that I had already studied intensively for my dissertation. Bergier completed the transcription of that volume and then prepared one of the entire first volume. Dufour, at that time an employee of the Librairie Droz, checked our work out carefully and saw it through the press. These two volumes were duly published in 1962 and 1964. The three of us prepared a transcription that I believe has stood the test of time. I have not as yet discovered any errors in it. Some of our notes, to be sure, could be more complete. A few of them even contain silly errors. But the transcription itself still stands. This edition was the single most important reason, incidentally, explicitly offered for the award I received from the University of Geneva in 1986 of an honorary degree, docteur ès lettres honoris causa. That honorary degree, as you can see, was not earned by me alone. It was also earned by my teachers, Geisendorf and Vaucher, and by my collaborators, Bergier and Dufour. The experience taught me that a good edition of sixteenth-century manuscripts requires expertise in paleography. But it also persuaded me that it is best undertaken with the cooperation of several experts. This is not the kind of enterprise that is best tackled by a single scholar working all by himself. It really needs a team.

The work I did on that edition proved to be ideal preparation for my further work with French manuscripts. It provided a good introduction to French paleography. The section of the volume of the registers of the Geneva Company of Pastors which I edited had been transcribed by four different pastors, each with his own distinctive handwriting. One of these pastors had a fine Italian hand, a beautiful version of humanist handwriting that was very easy to read. The others were more difficult. The most difficult was by a man named Nicholas Colladon. I became a particular specialist on his hand.

This project also provided a good introduction to problems in annotating a text of this period. I found it particularly important and challenging to prepare footnotes establishing the identity of people mentioned in the text, above all, of course, of my 'missionary' pastors. I discovered that it is often especially difficult in a manuscript of this period to establish the paleographically correct spelling of a proper name, and that if one can find the same name in another source it may be of help in establishing the best of several possible spellings of that name. If one then wants to do something more with the person mentioned in the source that creates further reasons for establishing his identity more fully. One of my favourite examples in the text I was editing was a 'missionary' pastor named 'Le maître de Jussy.' This opened up two possibilities. The man could carry the not uncommon name of 'Lemaître' and come from the town of Jussy, quite close to Geneva. Or he could be 'the master' assigned to teach in the school in that town. When I explored the first possibility, I drew a blank. When I turned to the second, I hit the jackpot. One of the archivists brought to my attention a packet of pay receipts, countersigned at the time of the quarterly distribution of salaries by every individual on the payroll of the Genevan government for that period. The man who was then on the payroll as schoolmaster in Jussy turned out to be a man named Bernard de Prissac, who did in fact in later years exercise a ministry in the part of France to which 'Le maître de Jussy' had been assigned.[2]

The three of us who edited the registers of the Geneva Company of Pastors for the period of Calvin's ministry did not continue our collaboration. But the project still continues, now for the period after Calvin's death, a period which did not interest the philanthropist who got us started. M. Dufour, in collaboration with Louis Binz, the successor to Geisendorf as Professor of National History at the University of Geneva, in 1966 obtained a grant from the Swiss Fonds National de la Recherche Scientifique to make possible the edition of these registers for this later period. It was designed to complement another edition project, upon which M. Dufour was working in collaboration with Professor Henri Meylan of Lausanne, of the complete correspondence of Théodore de Bèze, Calvin's successor as Moderator of the Geneva Company of Pastors and leader of the international Reformed movement. That project had been underway for decades and was now also being supported by grants from the Swiss Fonds National de la Recherche Scientifique.

For the continuing edition of the registers of the Geneva Company of Pastors, MM. Dufour and Binz have trained and supervised younger scholars who have done most of the actual work of transcription and annotation, many of whom have moved on to other positions of distinction themselves. They projected continuing the edition throughout the relatively long career of Bèze and beyond, down to 1618, the date of the meeting of the Synod of Dort, an important turning point in the history of Calvinism. The Swiss grants supporting this project and the Bèze correspondence edition have been routinely renewed ever since, in a display of constant and continuing support of the work of editing scholarly texts that can only fill with envy those of us who work in North America. They have made possible ten additional volumes of the registers of the Company of Pastors, all of them larger and more fully annotated than ours, which take the series down to 1613. A thirteenth volume is now in preparation.

I had also wanted, for a long time, to see an edition of the registers of the Consistory for the period of Calvin's ministry. This is a bigger and more difficult project than the edition of the registers of the Company of Pastors. The Consistory registers are far more voluminous. It would take for the Consistory about ten fat volumes of about five hundred pages each to cover the period which the edition of the registers of the Company of Pastors covers in two volumes of less than two hundred pages each. And the handwritings of the Consistory scribes are notoriously difficult. These scribes were writing at top speed during actual sessions, and their handwritings degenerated into a stenographic scrawl almost like shorthand. There were four of them for the period of Calvin's ministry. One of them had a fairly legible hand, but unfortunately he held his secretarial job for only one year, and his successors were as bad as his predecessors. That is the obvious reason that almost all previous work on the Consistory has been based on the Cramer transcripts, not on the original registers themselves. As I have studied the Cramer transcripts, however, I find uses of them seriously flawed. These transcripts include only about five per cent of the total cases heard by the Consistory. They are shaky paleographically, with passages omitted without indication when Cramer could not decipher them. And, worst of all, they focus on the more spectacular cases and ignore the ordinary cases. They provide a seriously distorted view of the Consistory's operations. The attempt by one scholar, for example, to use these transcripts for creating statistics of the numbers of Consistory cases ending in different types of punishment is not worth very much.[3]

Over the years I had written a number of articles urging that someone edit the registers of the Geneva Consistory. Nobody responded to my appeals. Finally I decided I would have to do it myself. I had the good fortune to discover that the Meeter Center for Calvin Studies in Grand Rapids, which already had in its custody microfilm copies of these registers, was expanding its operations and looking for good projects. In 1986, I persuaded its board of directors to earmark funds for a transcription of all twenty-one manuscript volumes of these registers, beginning in 1542, soon after the Consistory first began its operations, ending in 1564, on Calvin's death. A student of mine who had just earned his PHD, Jeffrey Watt, now of the University of Mississippi, began the work of transcription. He had learned his French paleography in much the same way I had, in the Neuchâtel State Archives, from its director, Maurice de Tribolet, a graduate of the Ecole des Chartes. I helped him myself in these early stages. Then we both trained others to carry the project on. Watt trained his own new wife Isabella, who has become very expert at these hands and has been working nearly full time on the project since 1988. I trained several additional graduate students, most notably Thomas Lambert, who elected to write a doctoral dissertation for the University of Wisconsin-Madison using these registers, who acquired supplementary training in French paleography from Bernard Barbiche of the Ecole des Chartes, and who has worked for more than two years in Geneva.[4] Two other graduate students of mine, Glenn Sunshine, now of Central Connecticut State University, and David Wegener, also worked on the project. We have also been helped at several points by Gabriella Cahier and Alain Dufour of Geneva, who have checked parts of our transcriptions. This team has completed a transcription of all twenty-one volumes. Electronic copies have been forwarded to several scholarly libraries and are now being used by graduate students in such places as St Andrew's University in Scotland and the Princeton Theological Seminary in the United States.

Our transcription, however, is necessarily somewhat rough. It contains many lacunae and dubious transcriptions. It can only be used with considerable caution. So I wanted to go a step further. I wanted to prepare a true critical edition, with a text established as carefully as possible and accompanied with a full annotation. I wanted to do for the registers of the Consistory what was being done for the registers of the Company of Pastors. Fortunately the University of Wisconsin-Madison, which had helped to finance the transcription, has now put at my disposal funds that can be used to pay for work on the edition. By this time Thomas Lambert and Isabella Watt have become more expert in the hands of the secretaries of the Consistory than anyone else in the world. They are taking over the primary responsibility for preparing a critical edition of the first volume of Consistory registers. They have nearly completed the work of checking and annotating the text for an edition of this volume. Watt is now turning it into camera-ready copy. The Librairie Droz has agreed to publish it. It is my hope and expectation that this first volume will appear in the next few months, perhaps in 1995 or 1996.

The question no doubt should now arise as to why we are going to all this trouble. What is it within the registers of the Geneva Company of Pastors and of the Geneva Consistory that deserves all this labour and expense? The answers for the two series are quite different. The registers of the Company of Pastors provide a record of an institution that worked diligently to maintain the doctrinal purity of early Calvinism, to supervise the cycle of worship services within the Reformed Church of Geneva, and to encourage communities all over Europe, indeed as far away as Brazil, to adopt the Reformed faith. Bergier, in the volumes with which we began the series, edited extended records of the trials of Jerome Bolsec, who was accused of undermining Calvinist teaching on predestination, and Michael Servetus, who was accused of undermining orthodox Christian teaching on the triune nature of God and on a number of other matters. There are other records of both these trials, but our edition supplies valuable supplementary material for a full understanding of these important theological debates. I have also used these records for my own studies of early Calvinist attempts to evangelize France, in one book covering the period up through the first war of religion, in a sequel covering the period through the St Bartholomew's day massacres.[5] There are a number of similar studies these registers make possible.

The registers of the Consistory, on the other hand, provide a record of an institution that was a compulsory counselling service and a court, that tried to control in all its detail the behaviour of all the people in Geneva, that tried to make it certain that Genevans not only accepted true Christian belief but also led true Christian lives. When I first proposed the edition to one of my Genevan friends, he objected that these registers contain nothing but a dreary series of virtually identical fornication cases. They do indeed contain a good many fornication cases, and also cases of adultery and other sexual delinquencies. But they go well beyond sex to other kinds of behaviour. They reveal an institution resolved to make a community Protestant for the first time. They are full of detailed information on surviving Catholic religious practices and how the earliest Protestants tried to wipe them out or channel them in new directions. They show in intimate detail how this community was changed on the grassroots level, how the religious leadership of this community tried to turn ordinary people into Protestants, including many who were old and illiterate, including a high percentage (in some categories a majority) who were women. It thus gives us a fascinating cross-section of daily life at the very beginning of the Protestant Reformation. It shows us Calvin and his colleagues in action as pastors, not theologians.

To illustrate this point, let me now provide you with examples of some of my favourite Consistory cases. I would like to sketch three separate sets of them. The first involved a charge of sexual misbehaviour. The second involved ending a quarrel within a family with a formal reconciliation. The third involved popular understanding of an argument about some fine points of theology.

Among the cases involving sexual misbehaviour, my favourite is the record of the first fully documented divorce. It is a case that mixed in a way I find fascinating reports of sexual misconduct, reports on how preaching was understood, arguments on what type of law should be used to resolve a matter not covered by existing law, and considerations of how the community should handle someone who is mentally unstable. The case was brought before the Consistory by a man named Pierre Ameaux who wanted a divorce from his wife, Benoite Jacon. Pierre argued for this divorce on grounds that his wife had strange ideas, that she believed in adultery. Her reply was so incoherent that it immediately suggests the possibility that she was unstable mentally. In essence, however, she conceded that she did indeed believe that any Christian woman could sleep with any Christian man, because she had learned from the earliest Protestant sermons that we must all love our neighbours. The Consistory was shocked and referred Benoite to the city Council for punishment. The Council could find no evidence of actual adultery and referred her back to the Consistory with an order that she be reconciled with her husband. They were duly if somewhat forcibly reconciled. Several months later, Pierre returned and again demanded a divorce, now alleging that his wife had started actually to commit adultery. After several investigations, the Consistory and the city Council decided the charges were indeed true. The couple were duly divorced and Pierre got explicit permission to marry again. Benoite ended up confined at home in the custody of her relatives, the usual treatment for someone regarded as mentally ill. A divorce of this type had never been possible under Catholic law. In arranging for this divorce, the Consistory was responsible for an important innovation.[6]

Among cases involving the arrangement of reconciliations, my favourite is that of the Tissot family. Pierre Tissot was a distinguished and prosperous patrician, a member of Geneva's governing elite. He had been a member of Geneva's governing Council, he was at that time its state treasurer, he was to become one of its syndics or chief executives. His family problems were brought to the attention of the Consistory by his widowed mother. She complained that her illustrious son was neglecting her. He replied that he and his wife had supplied the elder Mme Tissot with a cash pension, stocks of grain, barrels of wine, and soup and medicine during her recent illness. She did not remember the soup and complained, repeatedly, that the wine was bad. She also complained that Pierre was neglecting his brother, apparently a younger brother, who was running wild and not settling down properly. I get the definite impression that Mme Tissot was approaching senility, getting old and forgetful, perhaps suffering from what we would call Alzheimer's disease. Her son Pierre and his wife solemnly promised to keep doing everything they could for his mother. After the details of a family understanding had been worked out in the Consistory, its members arranged for a formal ceremony of reconciliation which is described in the registers. It was held on a later day in a parish church in conjunction with a service. It was presided over by John Calvin and the lay syndic then serving as the presiding officer of the Consistory.[7]

Among cases involving popular understanding of fine points of Protestant theology, my favourites involve a group of supporters of Jerome Bolsec. Bolsec was a former Carmelite friar who had turned Protestant, who had come to the area around Geneva, and who supported himself as a physician, primarily to the family of a prominent refugee nobleman. But he remained interested in theology and in 1551 got himself into serious trouble for frontally attacking the Calvinist understanding of the doctrine of predestination. The attack occurred at a session of a 'congregation' or public meeting devoted to lay study of the Bible. It quickly turned into a highly technical exchange between Calvin and Bolsec on the exact meaning of a number of passages in the works of St Augustine, particularly in his anti-Pelagian tracts. Bolsec's manner so offended the authorities present that he was thrown into jail, intensively questioned on his understanding of predestinarian theology in the trial described in the registers of the Company of Pastors to which I have already alluded, found guilty of misbelief, and banished from Geneva. During the trial, a number of local people were called before the Consistory and questioned closely because they had been heard to say in public things that made the authorities suspect that they supported Bolsec. The record of that questioning provides very interesting insights into what ordinary people understood about this highly technical argument on predestination. Several of those accused of supporting Bolsec defended him for his character rather than for his ideas. They said he was a good man, that as a doctor he had cured many people. One woman reported that he had cured her of an annoying breast problem. For these people character took precedence over belief. They did not think that a man who did good things should be persecuted for his ideas. Others who supported

Bolsec saw him as the victim of a personal vendetta with John Calvin. They felt that Calvin was determined to force everyone in town to accept his version of Christian belief and was out to make trouble for anyone who disagreed with him. Some who supported Calvin, incidentally, also saw the quarrel in terms of a personal vendetta, but had such faith in the rightness of Calvin's positions that they believed he should not have to face rude contradiction. All of those summoned accepted the general Protestant principle that theological arguments must be resolved by appeal to Scripture, but several of them noted that Bolsec and Calvin both cited Scripture and they happened to find Bolsec's citations more convincing. None of them had a thing to say about the appeals to St Augustine and his anti-Pelagian tracts. I doubt that any of them understood these allusions. Only a few understood in a general way that the argument between Bolsec and Calvin was about the absolute power of God. One or two of them had absorbed Bolsec's argument that the Calvinist view could be interpreted as making God the ultimate source of evil, and they found that unacceptable. All were forced to recant their views and go on record as accepting the official theology of the Reformed Church of Geneva.[8]

These cases supply only a small foretaste of the results of the edition upon which we are working of the registers of the Geneva Consistory. I hope they have persuaded you that this edition, as well as the earlier and ongoing edition of the registers of the Geneva Company of Pastors, are worth doing.

NOTES

1 *Notes extraites des registres du Consistoire de l'Eglise de Genève, 1541–1814,* ed F.-A. Cramer (Geneva 1853).

2 Robert M. Kingdon and Jean-François Bergier eds, *Registres de la Compagnie des Pasteurs de Genève au temps de Calvin,* vol 2 (Geneva 1962) 92, note 4.

3 Walther Köhler, *Zürcher Ehegericht und Genfer Konsistorium,* vol 2 (Leipzig 1942) 614, note 544.

4 The working title for this dissertation is 'Popular Piety in Calvin's Geneva,' and Lambert hopes to finish it in 1995. Lambert has also arranged to publish two articles using some of this material: 'Cette loi ne durera guère: inértie religieuse et espoirs catholiques à Genève au temps de la Réforme,' to appear in the *Bulletin de la Société d'histoire et d'archéologie de Genève,* and 'Lampe du fidele ou fables des prédica-

teurs: les generois assistent au sermon au seizième siècle,' to appear in the *Revue de Vieux Genève*.

5 Robert M. Kingdon, *Geneva and the Coming of the Wars of Religion in France, 1555–1563* (Geneva 1956), and *Geneva and the Consolidation of the French Protestant Movement, 1564–1572* (Geneva 1967).

6 An extended discussion of this case will be found in Robert M. Kingdon, *Adultery and Divorce in Calvin's Geneva* (Cambridge, Mass. 1995) 31–70. I have also supplied shorter reports on the same case as a chapter titled 'The First Calvinist Divorce,' in Raymond A. Mentzer, *Sin and the Calvinists: Moral Control and the Consistory in the Reformed Tradition* (Kirksville 1994), and as a conference paper titled 'How one Genevan reacted to Calvinist Preaching: the case of Benoite Ameaux,' in Peter de Klerk, *Calvin and the State* (Grand Rapids 1993) 47–55.

7 See the fuller account in Robert M. Kingdon, 'The Geneva Consistory in the time of Calvin,' a chapter in Andrew Pettegree, Alastair Duke, and Gillian Lewis eds, *Calvinism in Europe, 1540–1620* (Cambridge 1994) 28–31.

8 For a fuller report on these cases, see Robert M. Kingdon, 'Popular Reactions to the Debate between Bolsec and Calvin,' in Willem van't Spijker ed., *Calvin, Erbe und Auftrag: Festschrift für Wilhelm Neuser zu seinem 65. Geburtstag* (Kampen 1991) 138–45.

J. DANIEL KINNEY

3 On Transposing a Context: Making Sense of More's Humanist Defences

The problems that More's texts present are extremely diverse and the genre to which they belong, or we claim they belong, is not much less so. It may be, nonetheless, that this very diversity makes More's humanist letters in our presentation especially useful examples of the working assumptions which characterize all the More Project's volumes, beyond that, the whole business of critical editing in its current phase of constructive debate and unsettledness.

My discussion of volume 15 of *The Complete Works of St. Thomas More* (New Haven 1963ff., cited as CWM in the following) which contains the bulk of More's humanist defences, will proceed from more abstract to less and from global to local reflections in a bid to make adequate sense of More's text. In the overall course of my talk I shall relate my own work with these texts to more general debates about critical editing in a form I would like to defend as a bona fide hermeneutic spiral, not just the old circle, in which the pursuit of definitive readings, no less than definitive meanings, is all too apt to run on and down. In my own case, establishing texts had to start with *defining* those texts both generically and materially in a way that essayed to do justice to a certain embarrassing richness if not out-and-out baffling exuberance of pertinent evidence in both those dimensions. For instance, it would quite clearly not do to class any of these generally long, generally formal, rhetorically organized texts as a 'letter' in our sense *tout court*, even though our generic conception of letters is quite Protean enough in its own way. In this sense, an already weak, loose account of one pertinent genre, the letter, in terms of expressive and formal affinities seems to need still more weakening before it can stretch to accommodate these texts by More. Indeed lumping More's humanist defences with all his other letters in Latin and English as if one frame of reference could be made to serve equally well for them all clearly caused serious problems for Rogers' 1940 edition of More's correspondence and the earlier Yale English renderings to which it gave rise. Although the letters in Allen's great critical text of Erasmus' correspondence are perhaps quite as heterogeneous as More's, the sheer bulk of the letters in Allen's edition supports a great deal more refinement by way of cross-reference and simple redundancy in the codes Allen uses to do justice to this same diversity. The particular scope of her work compelled Rogers to give these five defences editorial short shrift as a group. Recognizing that it would be hard to do justice to them in the welter of critical problems presented by More's other letters is what prompted Clarence Miller, the More Project's executive editor, to put these five Erasmian and humanist defences in an editing class by themselves and assign them to me.

Letter-writing stylistics in *our* terms aside, there is certainly no lack of conspicuous occasional or functional and topical links between these unfamiliar epistles of More's. Indeed, they tend to get cited or published together, or bound with other germane 'open letters' by More's fellow-humanists, almost from the start. Family ties or contextual links more than family resemblances (though undoubtedly there are resemblances too) are what first brought the More Project's Richard Sylvester and other More scholars far back in the sixties to start treating More's humanist defences as a unit, most of all the five 'public' epistles to Dorp, Oxford University, Lee, Batmanson, Brixius (de Brie). Yet these same family ties implicate the texts so much in topical controversy that a more natural linkage might well be with quite different texts, some by quite different authors, aligned less by expressive or formal affinities or indeed by a single shared author than by the sheer fact that each of the texts in the group bears in formative ways on a single historic dispute. This is certainly not just a formatting-cavil against single-author editions of topical texts, for remarkably even Clarence Miller himself chose to privilege a topical link over linkage by author or genre at one crucial point in directing the Yale Press edition of More's Latin poems. Three extensive appendices in volume 3/2 bearing on More's contention with Brixius include Brixius' two pamphlets in verse and More's own long prose letter-response, yet exclude an allied open letter addressed to Erasmus which might readily be classed as one more long and artful Erasmian or humanist defence were it not that it holds several lines deemed by some unbecoming to More as a humanist. This long letter (No. 1087 in Allen) is less missed than the quite different writings of Brixius would be in the topical context of this More appendix. Consequently, although More once announced plans to publish an omnibus volume including his Brixius epigrams, the two long poems by Brixius, and both More's long responses in prose, the broad compromise-scheme of the Latin-poems volume which joins linkage by author with topical linkage in its final part, still stops well short of a total adherence to More's own (at least short-term) intent.

In the spirit of the topical scope of new cultural studies (for example *Erasmus, Man of Letters*, that assertively *au courant* study by Lisa Jardine), one might also productively edit a whole volume of humanist texts bearing mainly on Dorp and his quarrel with Erasmus. Alternatively one might reprint the omnibus volume of letters defending Erasmus against Edward Lee from which we draw More's own lengthy letters to Lee and a Monk.[1] One might also combine More's quite frequently parallel letters to Dorp and a Monk with Erasmus' own texts in defence of revising the Vulgate; or one might join the humanist defences with the program-epistles from More's other humanist writings: for example, the brief letter to Gonnell sketching humanist training within More's own household or his program-epistles on humanist poetics introducing his Lucian and *Utopia*. Finally, we could – and did – invoke still broader humanist stylistic concerns to make sense of our ad hoc decision to publish along with the humanist defences the clean and remarkably rich Latin working-recension of More's *Richard III* I turned up in the course of preparing the texts I had actually set out to edit.[2] Thus the physical placement of these five defences in volumes 15 and 3/2 situates them for all their generic affinities in at least three quite different relations to More's other texts: as ancillas or paratexts rather like the various *parerga* of *Utopia*; as long letters which earn serious notice as more or less free-standing draft-manifestos for a humanist historical criticism and Erasmian cultural reform; and at last as a humanist *opus* in four or five parts fit to balance the second Yale text of More's *Richard III*, the great unfinished work which may well in its way be the more penetrating and searching engagement with humanist values that More ever attempts. Far from settling the question of these texts' generic identity our approach may appear to have heightened generic perplexity; yet it may be that this very heightening amounts to a cautious first step toward a bona fide measure of textual control, making sense of More's text without losing More's thread in a textual domain where, as More loves to stress (and a style of redundancy-coding for More confirms), *less* assurance is *more*.[3]

I am occasionally asked how I chanced on an overlooked *Richard III*, in the Bibliothèque Nationale, of all places. How was it overlooked for so long? It was bound, and thus indexed, as well, with a manuscript mainly in French. No one else, it seems, looked for Latin humanist manuscripts among the French *Fonds*. In the course of two weeks mainly spent below decks scanning old printed manuscript catalogues in Yale's Sterling Library I at last turned up one other major More manuscript which is by all means quite as intriguing as this, but much harder to handle. Property of the ill-indexed Cambridge University Library and tracked down at long last by an *Incipit* drawn straight from More, that text waits and may wait a long time for an editor really prepared for so tangled a job.

The heterogeneity of the humanist defences is also borne out by their very material diversity. Briefly noting the various material character of the texts on which we must rely helps us know More's defences by way of the company they keep, mostly company already described in my comments on linkage and genre. All the humanist defences but the *Letter to Lee* have appeared at some point in free-standing editions. The *Letter to Dorp* exercised a large influence even in manuscript and was eventually printed five times in conjunction with Erasmus' *Praise of Folly*. It represented a strikingly outspoken Erasmian program which earned it a place on successive indices. Although it is by far the most frequently reprinted of any of the humanist defences, it is telling how far from 'established' in absolute terms its texts is and seems bound to remain. Shifting readings are all integral parts of the show, however, and to baulk at the shift may well be to mistake the whole point of the process involved. What I have in mind here is Paul Zumthor's account of *mouvance* (non-authorial dissemination of readings) in essentially free-floating medieval manuscript texts.[4] As opposed to Erasmus' increasingly vigilant authorial control over his printed texts More appears to have paid less attention to this whole dimension of print-culture authorship after his first attempts to fix every detail in the print-presentation of *Utopia* both in two previous texts and in Froben's edition of 1518. His excuse in the year 1520 for the errors of scansion attacked by Brixius comes quite close to dismissing live authors' controlling directives, at least on fine points such as scansion, as if, living or dead, whether writing for scribes or the press, every author were equally subject to random *mouvance*. And though he once suggests he would gladly burn some of his own earliest works if they ever made their way into English he revealingly never provides clear instructions for either sorting or saving the rest of his works on the order of Erasmus' own careful instructions for disposing of his whole authorial legacy in the famous catalogue-letter addressed to John Botzheim in 1523.[5] Finally textualizing his life – and his death – perhaps more than the bulk of his writings, in what many perceived as the volatile medium of English than in the more settled, unaltering medium of Latin, making relics of some of his textual leavings merely by the renown of his martyrdom, More seems strangely pre-modern and post-modern at once in his ultimate indifference to a humanist print-culture's early ideal of near-total authorial sovereignty.

To turn back once again to material specifics and the textual families of More's *Letter to Dorp*. The first edition of the letter was a Basel collection of More's Latin writings from 1563. The source of the text seems impeccable since another long letter first published there (Allen's Ep 1087) is explicitly based on a copy from papers bequeathed by Erasmus to his printer-friends in Basel, and since we know that More sent to Erasmus in Basel both Dorp's long-unpublished second letter of cavils and More's own response. A textually related rough Sélèstat transcript of these same linked letters marked 'copied in Basel in 1518' also appears to be a direct descendant of the lost manuscript source. Yet the Basel recension of the *Letter to Dorp* contains both ill-digested additions and one seemingly deliberate omission unlikely to be More's own work. Thus this text seems to be a new draft of the text which Erasmus or one in his circle felt here and there free to revise. The second edition of the *Letter to Dorp – Dissertatio epistolica de aliquot sui temporis theologastrorum ineptiis, deque correctione translationis vulgatae Novi testamenti* (Leiden: Elzevir 1625; reiss. 'Sambix' [Elzevir], 1654) was a project engaging the two famous late-Renaissance Latinists Daniel Heinsius and Erycius Puteanus.[6] The readings of *1625* are remarkably close to the readings of our favoured manuscript *P* (Paris, Bib. nat. *ms.* lat. 8703). Both of these texts include a daring passage at page 76, lines 15–19, which both texts of the Basel recension omit at some cost to the sense. Furthermore, a conspicuous dash in the margin of *P* marks most points where the readings of *1625* differ even minutely from *P*, demonstrating that *P* was collated quite carefully at some point with *1625*. And at page 58, lines 28–60/1, where the correct reading is 'illa moralisatio quam vocant,' the scribe of *P* originally spelled the noun 'morilisatio' and then changed the first *i* to an *a* in a way that makes *r* look like *n* while the new *a* is not very clearly an *a* but still quite clearly dotted. At this point *1625* has the meaningless reading *monilisatio*. It appears that the copyist or editor misread the correction in *P* and admitted the meaningless 'monilisatio' on the strength of 'quam vocant' ('as they call it'), a phrase frequently used to apologize for an improper term borrowed from elsewhere. If we assume that the manuscript borrowed by Puteanus for this new edition was *P*, his remarks on the manuscript he borrowed lend additional credence to the evidence of an apparent address on the first leaf of *P*, and thus add to a fairly strong likelihood that this very manuscript, *P*, is the text More himself sent to Dorp; for as hard-pressed Puteanus is forced to point out, the text he needed back in a hurry from Heinsius was much-prized as a true family heirloom by someone from Dorp's own Louvain. Though a number of More's friends and relatives could conceivably have brought such a manuscript with them when they settled in Louvain as exiles, it is probably worth stressing that the recusant author Thomas Stapleton cites the *Letter to Dorp* from the Basel 'reforming' edition of More's Latin writings, and not from a manuscript text, even though he had privileged access to the most complete fund of More's letters brought over by More's exiled friends. *P* with *1625* lacks a number of more and less useful additions contained in the Basel recension. It is certainly not the last form of the text, but the one form that More in a clear sense released to its less-than-private first addressee. Should this then be the text that we actually print, accidentals and all, barring only quite grave and quite clear scribal errors, relegating the Basel additions to the textual apparatus and notes? That was my choice. Yet we know from More's autograph texts, for example, that one almost ubiquitous *tic* of *P*'s scribe, an insistence on marking almost every *e* as *ae*, almost never turns up in More's own Latin script, while More's own quaint recourse to not commas but virgules in Latin is no less at odds with standard usage in *P*. If this manuscript *was* sent to Dorp with More's substantive blessing despite such conspicuous stylistic discrepancies, all that we seem entitled to say about such accidentals is that More for one readily discounted them. In cases like these I felt quite free to standardize even *P*'s usage away from what merely distracts us from *P*'s basic soundness. Though the texts of the other defences stem from less numerous and less disparate sources (for example the letters to Lee and a Monk [Batmanson]), the main point of this lesson holds true for them, as well: what makes this text or that the 'definitive' text is not seldom in large part a function of what this or that new edition intends it to do.

I view myself less as an editor proper than as a student and would-be expounder of cultural contexts in general, contexts in the dynamic oppositional sense brought to bear on the old status quo, with momentous results, through the humanists' historical criticism. I refer at this point to Panofsky's well-known 'rule of disjunction'[7] now habitually invoked as a norm for distinguishing between piecemeal medieval absorptions of classical culture and the Renaissance bid to put it back together in all its unyielding distinctness. The first contexts addressed in my volume were naturally enough the historical contexts of More's humanistic defences, contexts even more amply examined in Erika Rummel's fine study, *Erasmus and His Catholic Critics* (Nieuwkoop 1989). What we need to know first to make sense of More's edited letters may not be what we need to know first to make sense of the way they were edited, but *mutatis mutandis* we need to have both sorts of context at ready – and not only these – to make adequate sense of the volume *in toto* no less than this sketch of its scheme. In what context was it worth More's while to take issue with Dorp at such length? What made Dorp, Lee, the anti-reformers at Oxford, the ignorant monk, or the witling Brixius worthy targets for More's style at all? Once we note the close topical and occasional links between More's answers to the first four of these targets, what earns More's forestalled personal dispute with Brixius anything like the same interest we are generally quite quick to confer on a fight for Erasmian principle? To be brief, when presented alone the historical contexts may yield adequate reasons for writing, but not for what More actually writes. Other cultural contexts explored in the three subsequent chapters of my introduction to volume 15 of *CWM*, entitled 'Christian Wisdom and Secular Learning,' 'Positive Theology and Erasmian Reform,' and at last 'Structure, Style, and More's Readers,' still to me seem to form a fairly *minimal* basis for doing justice to More's actual sense, even granting as I freely do that the sense we discern varies more than a bit with the contexts that we bring to bear on it.

The historical contexts of these five defences are easily summed up. As a pivotal figure in a pivotal scene for the spread of Erasmian humanism, Martin Dorp the Louvain theologian and sometime Erasmian was indeed all but fated to run foul of one camp or the other, or as he finally did, both at once. Possibly in large part to shore up his support in Louvain's theological faculty Dorp addressed two critiques to Erasmus in brief open letters in 1514–15. Erasmus answered the first at some length (Allen Ep 337) but got word of the second by way of More's lengthy response, written during More's well-known 'Utopian' embassy and completed in Bruges on 21 October 1515. It seems More's letter actually caused Dorp to reverse his position, though Erasmus, as if in return for Dorp's turning, arranged for More's letter to be left unpublished. The power of More's case against 'speculative' theology and for humanist Biblical scholarship prompted Juan Luis Vives to borrow large parts of More's opening arguments for his pamphlet 'Against the Pseudo-Dialecticians' of 1519; and More himself finally recast and published much else from the *Letter to Dorp* in his 1520 *Letter to a Monk*. The conservative presence in Louvain found a circle of like-minded allies in England among the supporters of Bishop Henry Standish in Oxford as well as at court. More's response to an anti-Greek faction at Oxford in his letter to Oxford University dated 1518–19 is the first of More's still-preserved written responses to an anti-Erasmian faction in England with ties to Louvain. Edward Lee, a young friend of More's family, pursued his own assault on Erasmus' New Testament from Cambridge to Louvain in 1517, publishing his lengthy list of ripostes to Erasmus' New Testament *Annotations* in a volume of early 1520. Almost at the same time, Lee's associates in England as well as Louvain launched more sweeping assaults on a whole range of works by Erasmus, assaults like the lost tract by the Carthusian John Batmanson to which More makes an equally sweeping response without naming his target in his 1520 *Letter to a Monk*. This long letter appeared with a far more restrained open letter to Lee; by combining the vehemence of one with the painstaking tact of the other More weakens Lee's cause perhaps more than he could have with merely one frontal assault. Though Erasmus himself chose to write off More's poetic feud with Brixius as no more than a personal squabble, the theory of fiction and humanist persuasion More advances to back up his earlier scoffs at Brixius' jingoistic absurdities has a rich and provocative bearing on humanist styles, literary and social alike. It quite clearly repays the close reading the More volumes' grand format invites.

On the subject of grand editorial formats I would like to point out a few quite different ways in which inclusive, intricate texts like the More Project's typically work. The Yale edition offers the Latin text with apparatus and, on facing pages an English translation. The text is preceded by head- and end-notes explaining the historical background and publication history as well as identifying ethical and contemporary references. What may look like a runaway mania for inclusion actually offers a whole range of codes, local genres or *topoi* among them, for what I call transposing a context. In this sense the Yale volumes set out in a fairly responsible fashion to 'have it both ways,' serving textual integrity no less than the needs of distinctly modern readers and contriving to be multivalent and clearly multipurpose without ever confessing to anything like dialogic intent. Volumes like ours are highly cohesive and highly distracting at once, though undoubtedly sometimes more one than the other depending on one's point of view. As a case in point I cite the still more extravagant format chosen by André Prevost for his edition of More's *Utopia* (Paris 1978) sporting no less than six different page-numbering systems and five reference-keys or what hypertext jockeys call 'buttons.' The editor's dilemma is well expressed by the ambivalence of the work 'editing,' a term routinely used in our culture to connote both refining and falsifying. Editing is habitually torn between two different rhetorics, between a rhetoric of textual improvement and a rhetoric of textual integrity, and the knack of the More Project's style is to satisfy – in a sense – both. In their argument as well as their form the five humanist defences are all more or less 'open letters,' and as such each plays off in an interesting way several different rhetorical contexts and modes of reception. The Yale text dramatizes and replicates this same diversity even as it presents or sets out to present the whole, integral text, paralleling in this More's own general ambivalence about the new medium of print and its mixed bag of consequences for textual dissemination and authorial control. It is not new to stress that the knowledge we need to make sense of a text is quite frequently context-specific, though as strictly occasional knowledge this is often quite comfortably relegated to the limbo or liminal 'background' of footnotes or commentary. Footnote-knowledge is even now I think frequently seen as an incidental irritant or, at the very most, a necessary evil, and until recently texts that required many footnotes for basic comprehension were as likely as not to be faulted esthetically in one of two ways, upwardly for affected allusion, or downwardly, for their failure to transcend or escape their immediate cultural context, for staying too 'implicated in matter.' Footnote-knowledge not readily assimilated in an opening interpretive survey or a general interpretive study can indeed seem inert and distracting by simple default, whence a widespread disdain of 'source-hunting' even among those most busied with 'influence.' The many intricate ways in which More's humanistic defences play off disparate contexts and codes in the course of one argument is not unlike the ways in which our volumes play at re-fracting and focusing meaning at once, at both triangulation and anamorphosis on two facing pages, at detailing an insistent material diversity face-to-face with a seamless abstract of More's up-to-date gist. Thus, in practice, at least, the edition sustains More's ambivalent stance with regard to authorial control, and like More, understands or essays making sense as a highly contextual exchange between more minds and viewpoints than one. As we start to display (as we do in these volumes) how More's ways with allusions operate to inform or mislead various readers about their own roles in the textual exchange then and now, we approach but with luck never more than approach that elusive horizon beyond which there is only our context.

NOTES

1 *Epistolae oliquot eruditorum* (Antwerp: Hillen 1520).
2 Cf my introduction to the textual history in CWM, volume 15, cxxxiii–cliv.
3 I refer to More's comment in the *Letter to Dorp* (p 94, lines 5–24) about Greek diacritical marks as prime entries for local transcription mistakes which are nonetheless also restraints on more general inaccuracy. This is much like that favourite idea of the new Information Theory, namely, that as the level of organization increases, potential disorder does too, but disorder now easily checked or contained thanks to that order's failsafe complexity.
4 For a similar model of the freeplay of readings in coterie verse for informal performance by Donne and his friends see the essay by Ted-Larry Pebworth 'MS Transmission and the Selection of Copy-Text in Renaissance Coterie Poetry,' forthcoming, TEXT 7.
5 CWE Ep 1341A.
6 Note for instance these phrases translated from the latter's two 1623 letters to Heinsius as excerpted in CWM 15, cxxi, note 1: 'The Elzeviers write me that they have sent you that More text to peruse. I am being pressured here [in Louvain] to return it, for the man treasures it like the old family heirloom it is. ... You don't know how keen I am to get those More items. The text by all means merits release, and with your supervision ...'
7 *Renaissance and Renascences in Western Art* (New York 1969) 85 ff.

ANNE M. O'DONNELL, SND

4 Editing the Independent Works of William Tyndale[1]

The reformer William Tyndale was born in Gloucestershire, between the port of Bristol and the university of Oxford, about 1494. After earning his BA and MA at Oxford, Tyndale probably studied at Cambridge where Erasmus had recently (1511–14) taught Greek and theology. Inspired by Erasmus' Latin translation of the Greek New Testament (1516) and Luther's German translation (1522), Tyndale sought authorization from the Bishop of London to make an English translation of the Bible. But the bishop declined permission because of links between vernacular bibles and heretics, both Lollards and Lutherans. By emigrating to Cologne, Worms, and Antwerp, Tyndale found freedom to get his biblical translations, polemics, and exegesis into print.

On the continent Tyndale published English translations of a complete New Testament (1526, 1534, 1535), Pentateuch (1530), and Jonas (1531). These translations occasioned original works of exegesis and controversy. *Parable of the Wicked Mammon* (1528) denied spiritual merit for good works. *Obedience of a Christian Man* (1528) prescribed absolute obedience to secular rulers except for ungodly commands. *Practice of Prelates* (1530) castigated Cardinal Wolsey's ambition and greed. *Answer to More* (1531) expounded Reformation principles in the first third of the book and rebutted More's *Dialogue Concerning Heresies* in the last two-thirds. *Exposition of 1 John* (1531) and *Exposition upon Matthew* (1533) praised authentic faith and gave pastoral exhortations.

Arrested and condemned for asserting justification by faith alone and rejecting papal authority, Tyndale was executed outside Brussels on 6 October 1536. His completed translations of the New Testament and the Old Testament through 2 Chronicles were included in every Protestant version of the English Bible from 1535 to 1611. His independent works were republished individually under Henry VIII and Edward VI and collectively under Elizabeth I. In the next decade they will be published by the Catholic University of America Press in a critical edition.

Like the Lord's Prayer, on which Erasmus and Tyndale both wrote commentaries,[2] this paper has seven sections: the history of the Tyndale Project; poststructuralist theory; the problem of authorship; problems with the colophon; the copy-text; editorial issues in individual books; later sixteenth-century editions of the independent works. Most of these sub-topics emerged inductively from the empirical data, but I also allude to the exchange between Roland Barthes and Michel Foucault on 'the author-function'[3] in tracing William Tyndale's gradual acknowledgement of an authorship which resulted in his execution for heresy.

I begin with the history of the Tyndale project. While the St Thomas More project was preparing the *Confutation of Tyndale's Answer* for publication in 1973, the executive editor, the late Richard S. Sylvester, laid the groundwork for an adjunct series on the works of More's opponent. Tyndale himself considered his biblical translations to be his most important work. Yet his vernacular translations and theological glosses aroused such opposition that he was prompted to compose in response polemical and exegetical tracts. These independent works are now available only in a reprint of the nineteenth-century Parker Society editions.[4] Their Victorian editor gave minimal annotations, paid little attention to early sixteenth-century linguistic developments, and removed references to bodily functions. By encouraging four of his graduate students to prepare critical editions of these treatises for their dissertations, Richard Sylvester formed a cadre of texts for the first scholarly edition of the independent works. The realization of this project encountered a number of obstacles, however.

Sylvester's premature death in 1978 deprived us of a friend and patron. Yale University Press, the publisher of the More project, declined to take on Tyndale as a companion project because it was already committed to a number of critical editions: the papers of Boswell, Johnson, Walpole, and Franklin. Negotiations were under way with Duke University Press when we discovered that a British press claimed to be working on a new edition of Tyndale. Thus in July 1981, Duke withdrew its tentative agreement, and progress on a critical edition of Tyndale came to a halt. This British edition of Tyndale never appeared.

In October 1986, the four-hundred-fiftieth anniversary of the death of Tyndale, I asked the director of the Catholic University of America

Press about the possibility of their publishing the works of St Thomas More's opponent, but wondered about the eligibility of Tyndale, given the Catholic mandate of the press. Dr David McGonagle assured me, however, that the press was concerned with sound scholarship, not religious affiliation, and that the publication of Tyndale texts would no doubt illuminate the writings of More. In October 1986 I succeeded John A.R. Dick as Executive Editor, and the Tyndale Project was established at Catholic University near the Folger Shakespeare Library. Such is the history of the founding and re-founding of the Tyndale Project. Care was taken in assembling a well-balanced team of collaborators. Because all the original editors were formally trained in literary scholarship, a special effort has been made to find scholars trained in church history to serve as theological co-editors for each text. An Advisory Board of scholars associated with the More, Erasmus, and Hooker Projects has been formed to give general support and advice on specific occasions. Each volume of the independent works will be submitted for official approval to a committee of the Modern Language Association of America.

The purpose of the edition, named *The Independent Works of William Tyndale*, is to present the texts, excluding biblical translations, for the use of specialists in the fields of English literature, history, and theology. Following the procedures of the More Project, the texts will be given in their original spelling and punctuation; however, all abbreviations will be expanded except for the ampersand (&). Unlike the More volumes, where each introduction is virtually a monograph, practical considerations limit the size of the Tyndale volumes, which will therefore be accompanied by succinct introductions. Discussions of issues connected with the texts, such as Tyndale's use of Scripture and Tyndale's attitude toward the law, have been published separately.[5] Others, which were the subject of papers given at a conference at Washington, DC, in July 1994 and at Oxford in September 1994 will also be published.

The following principles have been adopted with regard to the text: as will be explained below, the first edition of Tyndale's texts has proved authoritative for all of the *Independent Works* and thus will serve as the copy-text. An appendix, 'Historical Collation,' will record all substantive variants from later sixteenth-century editions, usually printed with government approval in London. Each work will have an index citing Tyndale's quotations from the Bible, his source *par excellence*. The commentaries will annotate biblical sources, will provide theological cross-references to Erasmus, More, and Luther, and explain major historical references and linguistic developments. Because the early sixteenth century marked a period of transition in the history of the English language, the glossaries will note obsolete words and senses, as well as first usages of new words and senses. Although a critical edition of Tyndale's biblical translations is beyond the scope of the project, Tyndale's prefaces to the biblical books that he translated will be included.

In his recently published biography of Tyndale, David Daniell generously acknowledges our work-in-progress: 'An admirable Tyndale Project based in Washington, DC, will in the next years produce, in four finely edited scholarly volumes, the works of Tyndale. But those "complete works" do not include the Bible translations' (Daniell 5).[6] Daniell has inadvertently conflated the title of Yale's *Complete Works of St Thomas More* with Catholic University's *Independent Works of William Tyndale*. Although we recognize that Tyndale's biblical translations are his major achievement, we have limited this project to the independent works and hope that scholars with the proper expertise in the biblical languages will accept the challenge of preparing a critical edition of Tyndale's scriptural translations.

The Catholic University Edition aims to publish four volumes in a press-run of five hundred copies each. Our intended audience is found in universities and divinity schools, pursuing graduate and post-doctoral studies. Although we originally considered publishing a paperback anthology for undergraduates, others are already addressing the need. David Daniell is preparing a modern-spelling version of *The Obedience of a Christian Man* for Penguin Books. Matthew De Coursey has been commissioned by the Centre for Reformation and Renaissance Studies, Victoria College, University of Toronto, to prepare a modern-spelling version of selections from the polemics between More and Tyndale. We welcome these efforts to present modern-spelling versions for the general reader, while we labour to complete the old-spelling critical editions with full commentaries for specialists.

Although Tyndale is an early modern author, viewing his works from a poststructuralist vantage yields fruitful insights. In his classic essay 'From Work to Text,' Barthes distinguishes the two thus: 'The work closes on a signified. ... The Text, on the contrary, practises the infinite deferment of the signified ...' (158).[7] Perhaps inspired by this antithesis, D.F. McKenzie in his *Bibliography and the sociology of texts*,[8] posits an analogous distinction between closed and open texts (McKenzie 51): 'closed' means 'authorially sanctioned, contained, and historically definable'; 'open' means 'always incomplete, and therefore

open, unstable, subject to perpetual re-making by its readers, perform-
ers, or audience' (McKenzie 45). Since Barthes asserts, 'it would be
futile to separate out materially works from texts' ('From Work to Text'
156), he probably would disapprove of separating closed from open
texts. Nevertheless, for heuristic reasons, I will consider Tyndale's
Independent Works as closed and his biblical translations as open texts.

The two concepts of text are analogous to two concepts of author:
author, autonomous and collaborative.[9] Generally speaking, Tyndale
is autonomous in his independent works. By 'autonomous' I mean that
Tyndale began and completed work on his subject matter and form
without major assistance. He asserts authorship of his own writings,
although implicitly acknowledging God's originary power. For example, he asserts authorship of *Introduction to Romans* and *Pathway into
Scripture* in *Exposition of 1 John*:

> And therfore ar there diuerse introductions ordeyned for youe / to
> teache youe the profession of your baptyme the only light of the
> scripture / one vpon the pistle of Paule the Romains and a nother
> callyd The pathe way in to the scripture. (*1 John* A7V, PS 2:144)[10]

In *Obedience* (I2V, PS 1:223 and Q3V, PS 1:296),[11] Tyndale refers to
Mammon, twice calling it 'my boke of the iustifienge of fayth.' In
Answer (H3V, PS 3:97; Q5, PS 3:200),[12] he cites *Mammon*'s discussion of
good works in James and Augustine. Twice he praises *Obedience*: in
Practice (K7V, PS 2:342)[13] for resisting Wolsey and in *Answer* (H3, PS
3:96) for opposing Fisher.

If Tyndale is an autonomous author in composing his independent
works, he may be labelled collaborative in making his biblical
translations. At first, Tyndale publicly named no author, neither
himself nor his assistant, William Roye, who helped with the 1525
New Testament in Cologne and the 1526 New Testament in Worms
(Daniell 109). Miles Coverdale helped with the Pentateuch in Ham-
burg, 1529 according to John Foxe (quoted in Daniell 198). By sharing
the burden of correction Tyndale enhanced the accuracy of his work.
However, unauthorized corrections were introduced by George Joye.
He changed 'resurrection' to 'life after this life' in twenty-odd places
in the fourth of the pirated editions of the 1526 New Testament
(Daniell 323–4). In protest, Tyndale put his name on the title page of
the 1534 New Testament to distinguish his translation from George
Joye's. This revised edition was the first biblical translation to carry
Tyndale's name on the title page (Daniell 325).

Probably because he was a fugitive, Tyndale's pre-publication manu-scripts have been lost. Perhaps they were confiscated when he was arrested in Antwerp, and permanently lost when that city was sacked in 1576 or heavily bombed in 1944. Thus we cannot study Tyndale's process of composition. '[R]ewriting of plays to meet the demands of performance,'[14] a Renaissance practice discussed by James Thorpe, is not confined to that genre. Tyndale was always willing to accept sug-gestions from his readership that would improve his biblical transla-tions. For example, he agreed with More's objection to the Latinate 'senior' in the 1525 New Testament and changed it to the Anglo-Saxon 'elder' in the 1534 New Testament (*Answer* A8, PS 3:16). But his in-dependent works present his own polemical or exegetical positions.

In his response to Barthes' ground-breaking article, 'The Death of the Author,' Foucault explains the birth of the author historically, 'Texts, books and discourses really began to have authors ... to the extent that authors became subject to punishment, that is, to the extent that dis-courses could be transgressive' (Foucault 108). This dictum could just as well be applied to Greek philosophers or Hebrew prophets, but we will limit ourselves to biblical translators. Tyndale gradually revealed his authorship of proscribed books, knowing such activity would prob-ably lead to his execution for heresy. In the preface to *Mammon* (1528), Tyndale reacted to the burning of his unauthorized English New Testa-ment (1526) thus: '[I]n brunninge the new testamente they did none other thinge then that I loked for / no more shal the[y] doo if they brunne me also / if it be gods will it shall so be' (*Mammon* A5, PS 1:43–4).[15] In Tyndale's case, his birth as an author led to his death as a martyr.

There are issues of authorship in each of Tyndale's individual pub-lications: those where the identity of the author is contested; those without any author identification; those where Tyndale asserts his claim to authorship by using either his full name or initials in the author's preface, on the title page or within the body of the book.[16]

First, there are three publications with problematic authorship: the 1525 New Testament Prologue, the 1531 *Answer to More*, and the anonymous *Enchiridion* published in 1533–4. Commenting on the 1525 New Testament, David Daniell suggests that the last five pages of the Prologue were written, not by Tyndale but by William Roye, 'the images and colloquialisms ... being coarser and the syntax rather more muddied' (Daniell 133).

After Tyndale attacked George Joye for publishing his own eschato-logical theology under Tyndale's name, Joye responded with his defensive *Apology*. There Joye asserted that the young reformer John Frith was the real author of *Answer to More*, 'Frith wrote tindales answers to More for tindale / and corrected them in the prynte / and printed them to at Amelsterdam ...'[17] Louis A. Schuster, one of the co-editors of More's *Confutation*, believes that Frith wrote much of the last third of the volume, that is, refutations of More's Books Three and Four (CWM 8, 3:1234 n. 3). No one contests the authorship of the first third of Tyndale's *Answer to More*, the critical foundational essay, where Tyndale sets forth his theological principles. If Frith did indeed collaborate with Tyndale, it is more likely that he worked on the last two-thirds, that is, all of the short chapters which respond to More's *Dialogue Concerning Heresies*, Books One to Four. However, in compiling the glossary for Tyndale's *Answer*, I found that the OED listed more than fifteen words used also by More (see below), but only half a dozen words used also by Frith. Ironically, Tyndale shares more vocabulary with his adversary than with his disciple. More important, Frith's *corpus* is noteworthy for its cogent material, clear organization, and annotated sources, most unusual for a sixteenth-century author. These characteristics are not in evidence in the *Answer* published under Tyndale's name. Therefore, I do not accept the hypothesis that Frith is the author of the later sections of that work. Perhaps George Joye confused Frith's *Answer to More* of 1533 with Tyndale's of 1531, although both were published at Antwerp not Amsterdam.[18]

The last work with a problematical authorship is the translation of Erasmus' *Enchiridion militis Christiani*, which, according to Foxe, Tyndale made while a tutor in Gloucestershire between 1522 and 1524. An anonymous *Enchiridion* was published in 1533 and republished in 1534 in a heavily revised version. This is the book I edited for my doctoral dissertation and published with the Early English Text Society in 1981. I discovered few correspondences between the Scripture quotations in the English *Enchiridion* and Tyndale's New Testament and Pentateuch, but many between the 1533–34 *Enchiridion* and the 1582–1609 Douai-Rheims version. The reason for this anachronistic correspondence is that the English *Enchiridion* and the Catholic Bible both translate the Latin Vulgate, whereas Tyndale translates the Greek or Hebrew original. David Daniell suggests the plausible thesis that the anonymous translator might be Nicholas Udall, the author of the English version of Erasmus' Paraphrases of Matthew, Luke, and Acts published in 1548 (Daniell 72).

Besides these three examples of problematical authorship, there are other publications which lack authorship marks: both the 1525 Cologne

Fragment (Matthew 1 to 22) and the 1526 Worms Complete New Testament lack a title page; the 1536 *Pathway into Scripture* gives no author's name.

Conversely we find explicit references to Tyndale in the prefaces of several of his works, because he wishes to claim responsibility for the subject matter presented. *Mammon* (8 May 1528) is the first work to bear the author's name. The heading of the Preface reads, 'William Tyndale otherwise called hychins to the reader (*Mammon* A2, PS 1:37).'[19] Tyndale gives his name here to distinguish himself from William Roye (Daniell 143–4), his collaborator on the 1525–26 New Testament and now co-author with Jerome Barlowe of a gossipy satire on Cardinal Wolsey, *Rede Me and Be Not Wroth*.[20] More, in his *Dialogue Concerning Heresies*, tentatively attributes the composition to Tyndale:

> [This is] a folysshe raylynge boke agaynst the clergy and moche parte made in ryme ... the boke is put forth namelesse / & was in the begynnyng rekened to be made by Tyndall. And whyther it so were or not we be not yet very sure. (CWM 6:291)

Tyndale puts his name on *Mammon* so that readers will not attribute to William Roye this serious explication of the doctrine of justification by faith.

The *Obedience* (2 October 1528) is the second book to have the author's name in the preface, 'William Tyndale other wise called William Hychins vnto the Reader' (*Obedience* A2, PS 1:131). Three books published in the early 1530s contain the author's initials in the preface: 'W T' as a running title in *Practice*, 1530; 'W. T. To the Reader' as the running title of the general introduction to the Pentateuch, 1530 and 'W T' as the running title of the preface to Deuteronomy; 'W. T. vn to the Christen reader' (A2) of *The Prophete Jonas*, 1531. The *Exposition of 1 John*, September 1531 and the 1534 Genesis have the author's initials 'W. T.' on the title page.[21]

The *Answer to More* is the first book to have Tyndale's full name on the title page. In addition, his last name or the initial 'T.' occur frequently in his response to More's Book Four. The later pages of *Answer* reads like the script for a debate between 'More' and 'Tyndale,' 'M.' and 'T.' Again, Tyndale's purpose is to claim responsibility for the subject matter.

Much more important than *Answer to More* is the revised New Testament of 1534. Here Tyndale's full name appears on the title page; his initials head the first preface; his full name, the second preface. The

Testament of master William Tracie published in 1535 also has the author's name on the title page.

To conclude this survey of authorial claims, I note that Tyndale's initials appear on the last page before the table of contents (p iii; missing from PS 2:132) in *Exposition upon Matthews*, 1533. Significantly, after Tyndale's execution for heresy, they appear between the canonical and apocryphal books of the Old Testament in 'Matthew's' Bible, 1537 (folio 94 verso). These large initials indicate Tyndale's hidden presence as the author of the English New Testament and Old Testament to 2 Chronicles in a book published under a pseudonym, John Rogers as 'Thomas Matthews' (Daniel 334–5). Indeed, all of Tyndale's completed translations were included in Coverdale's Bible (Zurich, 1535), Matthew's Bible (Antwerp, 1537), the Great Bible (1539), the Geneva Bible (1560), the Bishops' Bible (1568), and finally the King James Version (1611), which incorporated about 90 per cent of his work. Until the publication of David Daniell's modern-spelling versions of *Tyndale's New Testament* in 1989 and *Tyndale's Old Testament* in 1992, only a scholarly minority were aware of Tyndale's contribution to the English Bible.

It remains to comment on problems concerning colophons.[22] First, there are books that have no colophon: *Introduction to Romans*, Worms: Peter Schoeffer, 1526–27; *Answer to More*, Antwerp: Simon Cock, July? 1531; *Exposition upon Matthew*, Antwerp: J. Grapheus? 1533?

Another three have a false colophon: *Mammon*, 8 May 1528; *Obedience*, 2 October 1528; *Practice*, 1530. These books were supposedly printed by Luther's publisher, Hans Luft of Marburg. In fact, they were published in Antwerp by Johannes Hoochstraten, who printed Reformation books under an assumed name in Antwerp from 1526 to 1531. Hoochstraten published a dozen English books under this false colophon: Tyndale's *Mammon*, *Obedience*, Pentateuch, and *Practice*, and treatises by the Wycliffite John Purvey, Erasmus, Luther, and the reformers John Frith, Jerome Barlowe, and George Constantine. Outside this so-called 'Marburg Group,' the *Exposition of 1 John* has an incomplete colophon, giving only the date of 1531.

Crowning this list of sixteenth-century publications, the folio *Whole Workes* contains the full colophon, London: John Daye 1573. The revised STC notes that six copies have '1572,' the date on the title page, changed in ink to '1573.' Perhaps the folio was published between 1 January and 25 March, Old Style versus New Style dates for New Year's Day. In a forthcoming article,[23] John Dick notes that William Rastell's 1557 publication of the English works of More is answered by

John Foxe's edition of Tyndale, Frith, and Barnes: one Catholic opposed by three Reformation martyrs.

Let me now proceed to a discussion of problems encountered by the editorial team of the *Independent Works*. The first issue to be settled was the choice of a copy-text. Normally the earliest version is used.[24] Only one edition of each independent work was published before Tyndale's arrest and imprisonment ca. 21 May 1535 (Daniell 364). There were six later editions published in Tyndale's lifetime: the second edition of *Obedience*, 29 October 1535, Antwerp: H. Peetersen van Middelburch?, and five other editions published in England in 1536. It is not likely that Tyndale influenced the publication process from prison. Besides these further editions closely follow the first. Therefore, we will publish the texts that we consider to represent both the first and the final authorial intention.

The following editorial issues concern individual books. Tyndale's independent works include several short pieces and six major treatises. Two works survive in only one copy, *Introduction to Romans* with a brief commentary on the Pater Noster (1526), in the Bodleian; *Pathway into Scripture* (1536), in Emmanuel College, Cambridge. The presumed first edition of *Brief Declaration of the Sacraments* (1533?) is extinct. Therefore, editor John T. Day will use the 1548 edition as copy-text. Tyndale's original letters to John Frith in prison no longer exist. Day will therefore collate the copies from John Foxe's *Book of Martyrs* and the 1573 folio.

The first independent work to be published was *The Parable of the Wicked Mammon* (8 May 1528). The textual editor John Dick ('Posthumous Revisions')[25] judges that the eight sixteenth-century editions represent three stages of theological thought on justification by faith. Editions 1, 3, and 5 (1528, 1537, 1548) emphasize faith and put the notes at the end of the book where they function like an index (Daniell 170). Editions 2, 4, 6, and 7 (1536, 1547, 1559, 1561) move the notes into the body of the book as marginalia. The sixteenth-century editor has added new notes emphasizing works of charity as part of a covenant relationship with God. Edition 8, the 1573 folio, adds further marginalia, partly to help the reader find the place on a very long page, and partly to return to the theology of justification by faith. In John Dick's words, these marginalia are 'even more resolutely solafidean and anti-papal than Tyndale's own' ('Posthumous Revisions').[26] Because the first editions of Tyndale's books were published in the Low Countries and set by compositors who presumably did not know English, they are filled with typographical errors. At the conclusion of *Mammon*, Tyndale makes the following comment:

> Be not offended most dere Reader that divers thinges are oversene
> [overlooked] thorowe negligence in thys lytle treatise. For verely the
> chaunce was soch / that I marvayle that it is so well as it is. Moare-
> over it becometh the boke even so to come as a morner and in vile
> apparell to wayte on his master [Christ] which sheweth hym selfe
> now agayne not in honoure and glory / as betwene Moses and
> Helias: but in rebuke and shame as betwene two mortherars / to trye
> his true frendes and to prove whether ther be any faith on the erth.
> (*Mammon* 14v, PS 1:126)

Tyndale is confident that errors in the accidentals will not prevent the
substance of his message from being heard.

The second of the major independent works is *Obedience* (2 October
1528), which has been reprinted more than any other. There are eight
separate editions. It was, moreover, included in the *Whole Workes*.
David Daniell rightly asserts that 'it is Tyndale's most important book
outside his translations' (Daniell 223) because of its subject matter and
form. It is 'the first book in English about the political effect of
Scripture' (Daniell 244), dividing the subject into three main parts:
duties of subordinates to superiors, responsibilities of rulers to
subjects, and signs or sacraments (Daniell 221–36).

Although it is true that Tyndale organizes his material well (another
case in point is the foundational essay in *Answer to More*), there are
other contemporary writers who do it better: John Fisher in his English
sermons and Latin controversies, John Frith in his English controversies, and Sir Thomas Elyot in *The Book of the Governor*. Erasmus, by
contrast, does not give a logical cogency to his works; instead, he gives
a rhetorical urgency. It was judicious to put the *Praise of Folly* into the
mouth of Folly herself, and to cast his social criticisms of church and
family into the conversational form of the *Colloquies*. More, too, is apt
to rhapsodize, ranging freely from topic to topic in *Utopia, Dialogue
Concerning Heresies*, and *Dialogue of Comfort*.

As textual editor of *Obedience*, Anne Richardson has shown special
interest in Tyndale's spellings, particularly their indeterminacy. It is
difficult to decide whether certain unusual spellings are typographical
errors or a transcription of Tyndale's Gloucestershire dialect. Richardson notes characteristic spellings in *Obedience* which I have also found
in *Answer to More*, e.g.: 'bedgar' for 'beggar,' 'misheve' for 'mischeve,'
'wordly' for 'worldly.'[26] Because of her great sensitivity to language,
Richardson is alert to Tyndale's puns. She notes how '1573 restores
portmanteau words to their univocal state': 'bisshappes' (bishops +
mishaps) > 'byshops'; 'divininite' (divinity + ninny) > 'diuinitie';

'whorshepe' (whore + worship) > 'worship' (Richardson 395). Richardson has also alerted us to the lack of a typographical sign for exclamations in Early Modern English; the question mark therefore sometimes does double duty as an exclamation point.

The third of the major independent works is *Practice of Prelates* (1530). *Practice* has the most complex publishing history of all Tyndale's independent works. Alone among the English reformers, Tyndale agreed with Katherine of Aragon on the validity of her marriage to Henry VIII. In 1548–49 the London publishers, A. Scoloker & W. Seres, cut the material explicitly opposing Henry VIII's rejection of Katherine (H4V THROUGH K9, PS 2:319–43). In 1573, the editor John Foxe continued to omit Tyndale's support of Katherine but restored Tyndale's criticisms of Wolsey (K2–K9R). Distinguishing between Roman and Anglican bishops, Foxe changed the title to 'The practice of *papisticall* Prelates' [emphasis added]. All omissions were restored by Rev. Thomas Russell in 1831 and kept by Rev. Henry Walter in the Parker Society volume, 1849. Thus, the *Practice of Prelates* exists in three sixteenth-century versions (1530, 1548–49, 1573). Poststructuralists include authors, editors, printers, publishers, booksellers, book buyers, and readers in a 'collective authorship';[27] but the Tyndale Project will follow conservative editing principles. John Dick will use the 1530 *Practice* as his copy-text, but include these examples of editorial self-censorship in appendices. *Practice* does not need the complex presentation appropriate to such masterpieces as *Piers Plowman, Arcadia,* or *The Prelude.*[28] The Folger version of *Practice of Prelates* is bound with *Answer to More,* both copies formerly owned by the dramatist and polemicist 'Iohan bale.'

As textual editor, I know *Answer unto Sir Thomas More's Dialogue* (July? 1531) best of all Tyndale's independent works. Whereas *Obedience* has the greatest number of separate editions (eight), *Answer* has the fewest (one). I have collated the only four copies of this edition that still exist: in Washington, London, Cambridge, and Dublin.

It seems appropriate to begin my discussion of this work with an examination of David Daniell's disclaimer for the importance of More to Tyndale studies:

> It remains curious, to put it mildly, that the gravitational pull of Sir Thomas More has been allowed to distort Tyndale's orbit. ... Study of Tyndale is necessary to scholars of More, as More wrote so many black columns against Tyndale; Tyndale's reply was one short book. More is not vital to the study of Tyndale. (Daniell 4)

I offer a differing view based on three points: diction, ecclesiology, and power politics. Barthes notes that 'etymologically, the text is a tissue, a woven fabric' ('From Work to Text' 159). Indeed, the glossary of *Answer to More* shows that poststructuralism's emphasis on the warp and woof of intertextuality is true for the discourse between More and Tyndale. Compilers of the OED cite these two opponents as alternating users of half a dozen religious and philosophical terms, e.g.: 'amice' or 'shawl-like vestment worn between the tunic and the outer garment at Mass' (F5, PS 3:73) first recorded use by Tyndale in *Answer*, second by More in *Confutation*, 1532; 'dispicions' or 'disputations' (P8, PS 3:194), first recorded use by More in *Life of Pico*, ca. 1510; second by Tyndale in New Testament Prologue, 1526; third by More in *Dialogue Concerning Heresies*, 1529; 'silogismus' or 'syllogism' (H5, PS 3:100), earliest recorded uses in 1382, 1430, 1480; next recorded use by More in *Dialogue Concerning Heresies*, then by Tyndale in *Answer* and again by More in *Confutation*.

A further reason for asserting that More is important for Tyndale studies stems from More's cross-references to *Mammon* and *Obedience* in *Dialogue Concerning Heresies* (CWM 6, passim); to *Mammon, Obedience, Answer,* and *Exposition of 1 John* in *Confutation* (CWM 8, passim); to *Answer* in *Apology* (CWM 9, passim). In particular, More's attack on Tyndale's choice in his New Testament of 'congregation' not 'church,' 'elder' not 'priest,' 'love' not 'charity,' 'repentance' not 'penance' (CWM 6, 1:285–7) reveals fundamental differences between Catholic and Protestant ecclesiology. Finally, I believe that More's literary and political reputation gave an extrinsic force to his polemical attack that Tyndale's intrinsic learning and integrity did not offset. Thus More's opposition very possibly contributed to Tyndale's arrest and execution for heresy before he could translate the prophetic and wisdom books of the Hebrew Bible. Of course, a critical edition of the independent works aims to give Tyndale his rightful place in the galaxy of sixteenth-century luminaries.

David Greetham in *Textual Scholarship* (317)[29] lists four roles needed in making a critical edition: textual editor, annotations editor, glossarist, and indexer. Performing each of these roles led me to discover notable features in *Answer to More*.

As textual editor, I have found in the 1531 *Answer* one trace of the presence of a Flemish compositor. According to the OED, forms of 'sprecan' with 'r' did not survive past the mid-twelfth century. However, Tyndale's Antwerp compositor may have been influenced by Low German 'spreken' to give 1531's 'sprake,' which I have emended to *spake* (K6, 4, PS 3:127). In the 1573 folio, I have observed how faithfully John Foxe followed the first edition of *Answer*, mainly turning it into a modern-spelling version for Elizabethans. Although Foxe adds numerous marginalia, these agree with Tyndale's theological positions. For example, 1531's sidenote 'Masse' (H3) becomes 1573's sidenote 'Christes Supper & not Masse' (PS 3:97); 1531's sidenote, a pointing hand (H6v), becomes 1573's sidenote, 'The Pope selleth sinne and paine & all that can be solde' (PS 3:103).

Like Anne Richardson in *Obedience*, I have puzzled over indeterminacy of spelling in *Answer*, e.g., the meaning of 1531's 'clocke' rendered in 1573 as 'cloke.' The word occurs in a passage where Tyndale protests the abuses of clerical celibacy: 'The myst of it blindeth the eyes of the simple and begyleth them / that they can not se a thousande abhominacions wrought vnder that clocke' (*Answer* M8v, PS 3:155). Does this spelling indicate a medieval 'clock,' in which time is counted by the striking of bells? Or does it indicate 'cloak,' a 'bell-shaped cape'? Indeed, 'cloak' is derived from 'clock.' Having to make some decision, I finally glossed 'clocke' as 'cloak' because 'mist' and 'cloak' can both hide the abuse of clerical celibacy.

As annotator, I wonder if I fall under David Greetham's censure, 'Some editors ... seem to regard the establishment of the text as a comparatively trivial matter preceding the real purpose of the edition – the writing of annotations' (Greetham 368). I confess that I find researching material for the commentary to be the most interesting part of preparing a critical edition. Indeed, a commentary is necessary for an early modern theological text. In explaining Tyndale's aspiration to translate the whole Bible into English, David Daniell repeats the Reformation assertion, 'The bare text, if given whole, will interpret itself' (Daniell 141). At the Tyndale conferences in Washington and Oxford, I displayed page proofs of the plain text of my critical edition of *Answer to More*. On each occasion, people expressed the hope that Catholic University Press would publish a companion volume of notes. In my opinion, neither the Bible nor *Answer to More* can do without a full commentary.

The Bible is, indisputably, the most important source of *Answer*. Because every octavo page has three or four allusions, there are approximately a thousand biblical references in *Answer* that need annotation. Tyndale's most frequently used verse is Jer. 31:33 (quoted in Heb. 8:10 and 10:16), 'I will put my law in their inward parts, and write it in their hearts,' to use the words of the King James' Version of Jeremiah. This reference to 'the law written in our hearts' occurs twenty-three times in *Answer*, once each in *Mammon* and *Obedience*, three times in *Exposition of 1 John*, and four times in *Exposition upon Matthew*. This verse could well be taken as the key to Tyndale's theology: justification by faith enables us to love God's law and thereby keep it.[30] It must be conceded, however, that the same verse is one of the seven major biblical texts most frequently used by More.[31] However, More interprets Jer. 31:33 as 'a lawe wythout booke' (CWM 8, 2:753/10–11) to defend oral tradition against the reformers' *sola scriptura*.

In addition to annotating references to the Bible, to Tyndale's other works, and to More, I have given in the commentary many references to Erasmus. Because of his contact with powerful patrons and friends, the Dutch humanist was knowledgeable about English affairs. For example, in a letter of March 1523 to Pope Adrian VI, Erasmus advises restraint in the treatment of heretics, 'In former times, I agree, that is how the Wycliffite party was suppressed [by the knife and cautery] in England by the royal power; but it was suppressed rather than extinguished' (Ep 1352, CWE 9.439 and note). In *Obedience* (C4, PS 1:161–2, S4v, PS 1:316) Tyndale makes a direct reference to Erasmus' *Paraclesis* and his Paraphrases on Matthew and Luke. In the other works there are occasional reminiscences of the *Enchiridion*, *Praise of Folly*, *Julius Exclusus*, and *Colloquies*.

Because the *Independent Works* transcend traditional academic boundaries, the Tyndale Project needs the collaboration of both literary editors and church historians. James Thorpe surveys their contrasting practices, 'It is a commonplace to say that literary editing at the present time overemphasizes the preparation of the text, while historical editing overemphasizes the annotation of the text' (Thorpe, 'Diversity' 19).[32] But, Thorpe adds affirmatively, '[T]he tradition of literary editing and the tradition of historical editing have been merging' (Thorpe, 'Diversity' 22).

To complement my annotations on the Bible, Tyndale, More, Erasmus, and English history, Jared Wicks, the theological co-editor of *Answer to More*, has fully annotated numerous references to the Continental Reformation. To give only one example: Wicks explains Tyndale's polemical charge that priests could buy a license to keep whores (*Answer* C7, PS 3:40–1) by citing the schedule of fines for concubinage prescribed by the diocese of Constance. He further cites the condemnation of this practice by the Council of Basel in 1435 and the Fifth Latern Council in 1514, as well as Zwingli's opposition in July 1522. Wicks' identifications of sources and learned annotations comprise approximately one-third of the commentary to *Answer to More*.

Besides serving as textual editor and annotator, I have also acted as glossator. Based on the *OED*, the 850-word glossary includes: last recorded Medieval and first recorded Early Modern uses, specific references to *Answer*, and words not listed at all in the *OED*.

Suggesting a possible tie between the Lollards and Tyndale, I note three important theological words first recorded in Wyclif's New Testament, 1382: 'elder' (A8, PS 3:16) as a translation of New Testament 'presbuteros,' recorded first in Acts 15:6; used second in Titus 1:5, 1526 New Testament; 'felingefaith' (A6v, PS 3:13) as opposed to mere intellectual assent, recorded first in Js. 2:17; used second in Prologue to Pentateuch, 1530; 'iustifienge' (Q1, PS 3:195) or 'the action of making, proving, or accounting just,' recorded first in Rom. 4:25; used second in *Answer*, but not mentioned in the *OED*. Last recorded ca. 1450, 'schryuen' or 'confessed (referring to sins)' (O3, PS 3:172) is one example of the handful of words that occur later than the *OED*'s record.

From the hundred-odd words, phrases, senses, and forms used by Tyndale which occur earlier than the *OED*'s examples, here are two theological examples: 'Eare confession' (O3, PS 3:172) or 'auricular confession' (III. 16.) is recorded only in 1549; 'church' (A6v, PS 3:13) for 'the invisible number of the elect' (II. 4. c.) is first recorded in 1561. Here are two metaphorical examples of senses which antedate the *OED*: 'peperith' (L7v, PS 3:140) or 'seasons (referring to writing)' (6. b.) is first recorded in 1600; the proverbial phrase 'with out ryme or reason' (H1, PS 3:92) or 'without good sense' (3. b.) is first recorded in 1664.

Among the *OED*'s several quotations from *Answer*, here are two examples of vivid language originating with Tyndale: 'mowseth' (M6, PS 3:151) for 'tears like a cat with a mouse' (3.); the proverbial phrase 'goeth to potte' (I3v, PS 3:110) for 'cuts in pieces like meat for the pot' (13.). Although there are twenty-odd cases where the *OED* uses quotations from *Answer* to illustrate the development of words already recorded, I will mention only one: 'foresinnes' (I5, PS 3:112) or 'previous sins' (II. 4.). Among the dozen examples of Tyndale's coinages not found in the *OED*, again I mention only one: 'imageseruice' (G3, PS 3:82) or 'idolatry'; the cognate 'image-worship' is first recorded in 1628.

An Index of Proper Names, an Index of Biblical References, and possibly a topical index, in which every item with more than five references receives its own entry, complete the auxiliary material.

Having examined at some length the editorial issues in *Answer to More*, I turn briefly to *The Exposition of the First Epistle of John* (September 1531). Donald J. Millus notes how the London editors emend 'pope' to 'bishop of Rome' in the 1537 and 1538 editions, published after the Act of Royal Supremacy in 1534. Millus also notes omissions of references to Wolsey and More (dead in 1530 and 1535 respectively), to insurrection (reminiscent of the Pilgrimage of Grace, 1536), to Henry VIII's marital problems and to the Eucharist (Millus 183–6). These omissions are further examples of political self-censorship. All three separate editions emphasize the importance of the Scripture by putting the quotations from the Epistle in larger type and Tyndale's commentary in smaller; the 1573 folio gives the Scripture in roman type and Tyndale in gothic.

An Exposition upon ... Matthew (1533?) is Tyndale's last major independent work. Its literary editor, Stephen J. Mayer, asserts that the first edition of the book is 'remarkably well printed and free from error' (Mayer 295).[33] This is the first of the independent works to use roman type throughout, thereby facilitating the reading of its biblical teaching. The page format is its most remarkable feature. All six separate editions, as well as the 1573 *Whole Workes*, emphasize the importance of the Scripture by putting the quotations from the Sermon on the Mount in larger type and Tyndale's commentary in smaller; the 1573 folio gives the Scripture in roman type and Tyndale in gothic. The Folger's first edition is unattractively bound with two other religious tracts, but the second edition (1536a) like the *Exposition of 1 John*, has a modern black leather cover and gold edges.

All of these books were reprinted in the *Whole Workes*, a folio published in 1573 of which over fifty copies survive. In the approximately forty years since Tyndale first published his independent works, English words changed in form and spelling. Thus, Middle English 'ensample' became Renaissance 'example' and 'thorow' assumed a multiplicity of spellings before settling into the problematic 'through.' Except for *Practice*, the Daye folio is remarkably faithful to Tyndale's original editions.

I conclude my remarks on editorial problems with a brief comment on later sixteenth-century editions of the independent works. Apropos of D.F. McKenzie's observation that 'texts might be edited "creatively" for political purposes' (McKenzie 29), we know that non-authorial emendations were made for theological reasons, especially in Tudor England. I am indebted to John T. Day for calling my attention to a pattern of multiple republications in certain significant periods. Years in which the Protestant cause was advanced by legal events also witnessed an increased number of new editions of the independent works of Tyndale.

Five works were republished in 1536, the year in which the Re-formation-inspired Ten Articles of Religion were promulgated. Five other editions were republished in 1537, the year in which Matthew's Bible (mostly Tyndale's) was published. *Exposition of 1 John* was republished in 1538, when a Royal Injunction ordered an English Bible to be put in every parish church.

In the first two years after the death of Henry VIII, 1547–49, the Duke of Somerset used his office of Lord Protector to implement religious reform. In 1547, only *Mammon* was republished, but seven other Tyndale editions appeared in 1548, along with English transla-tions of Erasmus' Paraphrases of the Gospels. In 1549, the Book of Common Prayer was published, and Tudor priests were permitted to marry for the first time. Three new editions of Tyndale appear in 1549.

There were no republications of Tyndale's independent works dur-ing the 1550s, especially during the Catholic Restoration under Mary I (1553–58). During the early reign of Elizabeth I, there were four new editions: two in 1561, the year when Ambrose Dudley was created Earl of Warwick; two in 1564, the year when Robert Dudley became Earl of Leicester.[34] Of course, all these editions were recapitulated by the *Whole Workes* in 1573.

Conclusion

This review of bibliographical issues in William Tyndale's independent works reveals more complexity than one might first suppose. Although most of these works appeared in only one edition before the author's imprisonment, the marginalia of *Parable of the Wicked Mammon* and the body of *Practice of Prelates*, as John Dick as shown, had a complicated publishing history after Tyndale's death. Most notable is Tyndale's gradual acknowledgement of authorship: his full name appeared on the title page of the first independent work in 1531, *Answer to More*, and of the first biblical translation in 1534, the revised New Testament. My examination of a dozen sixteenth-century editions of Tyndale at the Folger Shakespeare Library – some in their original covers of brown, others in modern bindings of red, tan, or black – prompts me to return to editing these early English Reformation texts with renewed energy. In the *Paraclesis* Erasmus expressed a pastoral wish for vernacular Scriptures, 'And I would that they were translated into all languages so that they could be read and understood not only by Scots and Irish but also by Turks and Saracens.'[35] Tyndale used the new print technology to publish his English New Testament and Old

Testament through 2 Chronicles, of which his independent works are the polemical and exegetical by-products. Because of the on-going influence of his biblical translations, William Tyndale was the outstanding English author in the Age of Erasmus.

Bibliography of William Tyndale's Works

1. Biblical Translations

Matthew's Bible. Antwerp: M. Crom for R. Grafton and E. Whitchurch, 1537.
NT, Cologne Fragment. *The New Testament Translated by William Tyndale, 1525.* Facsimile. Introduction by Alfred W. Pollard. Oxford: Clarendon Press, 1926.
NT, Worms. *The New Testament, 1526.* Facsimile. Introduction by F.F. Bruce. London: Paradine, 1976.
The New Testament (1534). Edited by N. Hardy Wallis. Cambridge: Cambridge University Press, 1938.
The Pentateuch, Being a Verbatim Reprint of the Edition of M.CCCC.XXX. Ed. J.I. Mombert. Introduction by F.F. Bruce. Fontwell, Sussex: Centaur Press Ltd., 1967.
The Prophete Jonas. Facsimile. Introduction by Francis Fry. London: Willis and Sotheran, 1863.
Tyndale's New Testament. A modern-spelling edition with an Introduction by David Daniell. London: Yale University Press, 1989.
Tyndale's Old Testament. A modern-spelling edition with an Introduction by David Daniell. London: Yale University Press, 1992.

2. Independent Works

1 John. Millus, Donald J., ed. 'An Edition of William Tyndale's *Exposition of the Fyrste Epistle of Seynt Ihon.*' Diss. Yale, 1973.
Answer. O'Donnell, Anne M., SND and Jared Wicks, SJ, eds. *An Answere vnto Sir Thomas Mores Dialoge.* Washington, DC: Catholic University of America Press, forthcoming.
A Brief Declaration of the Sacraments. London: Robert Stoughton, [1548?].
Introduction to Romans. A Compendious Introduccion vnto the Pistle to the Romayns. Facsimile. The English Experience 767. Norwood, NJ: Walter J. Johnson, Inc., 1975.
Mammon. Dick, John A.R., ed. 'A Critical Edition of William Tyndale's *The Parable of the Wicked Mammon.*' Diss. Yale, 1974.

Matthew. Mayer, Stephen J., ed. 'A Critical Edition of *An exposicion vpon the v. vi. vii. chapters of Matthew* by William Tyndale.' Diss. Yale, 1975.

Obedience. Richardson, Anne Maureen, ed. 'A Critical Edition of William Tyndale's *The Obedience of a Christian Man*.' Diss. Yale, 1976.

Pathway. *A path way into the holy scripture*. London: Thomas Godfray [1536?].

Practice. Dick, John A.R. and James Andrew Clark, eds. *Practice of Prelates*. Typescript.

The Testament of master Wylliam Tracie. Antwerp: J. Grapheus, 1535.

Parker Society. Ed. Henry Walter. Cambridge: Cambridge University Press, 1848–50; rpt. London: Johnson Reprint Company Ltd., 1968.

PS 1. *Doctrinal Treatises [Mammon, Obedience]*.

PS 2. *Expositions [of 1 John; upon 5, 6, 7 Matthew] and ... Practice of Prelates*.

PS 3. *An Answer to Sir Thomas More's Dialogue ...*

Whole Workes. *The Whole workes of W. Tyndall, Iohn Frith, and Doct. Barnes*. London: John Daye, 1573.

The Works of William Tyndale and John Frith. Ed. Thomas Russell. 3 vols. London: Ebenezer Palmer, 1831.

NOTES

1 I wish to express my gratitude for the two semesters I spent as a Senior Fellow at the Centre for Reformation and Renaissance Studies, Victoria University, 1988–9. I am indebted also to a seminar in October 1993 at the Folger Shakespeare Library, 'Editing after Poststructuralism,' conducted by Professor Paul Werstein of the University of Western Ontario. Finally I want to thank John A.R. Dick, W. Speed Hill, Grace Ioppolo, Matthew DeCoursey, and the anonymous readers for critiquing earlier versions of this paper.

2 Erasmus, *Precatio dominica* (1523); Tyndale, *Exposition upon V.VI.VII. Matthew* (1533). Cf Anne M. O'Donnell, SND, 'English Commentaries on the Lord's Prayer, William Tyndale's *Exposition upon Matthew* and Margaret Roper's *Devout Treatise*,' in *William Tyndale, the Bible and the Tudor World*, Proceedings of the William Tyndale Conference, Oxford, 5–10 September 1994.

3 Roland Barthes, 'The Death of an Author,' in *Image – Music – Text* (New York: Farrar, Straus and Giroux, n.d.) 142–8; Michel Foucault, 'What Is an Author?' in *The Foucault Reader*, ed Paul Rabinow (New York 1984) 101–20.

4 Henry Walter, ed, 3 vols (Cambridge 1848, 1849, 1850; repr. London 1968). I will note references to the Catholic University edition by signature number and to the Parker Society edition as 'PS 1, 2, 3' with page number.

5 'Biblical Interpretation in the Age of Thomas More,' *Moreana* 106-7 (July 1991); *William Tyndale & the Law*, Sixteenth Century Essays & Studies 25 (Kirksville 1994)

6 David Daniell, *William Tyndale: A Biography* (London 1994). All references will be given parenthetically.

7 In *Image – Music – Text*, 155-64 (see above note 3)

8 The Panizzi Lectures, 1985 (London 1986)

9 Cf Steven Mailloux, 'The Rhetorical Politics of Editing,' in *Devils and Angels: Textual Editing and Literary Theory*, ed Philip Cohen (Charlottesville 1991) 129.

10 Donald J. Millus ed, 'An Edition of William Tyndale's *Exposition of the Fyrste Epistle of Seynt Ihon*' (Diss Yale, 1973); cited as *1 John*

11 Anne Maureen Richardson, 'A Critical Edition of William Tyndale's *The Obedience of a Christian Man*' (Diss Yale, 1976), cited as *Obedience*

12 Anne M. O'Donnell, SND and Jared Wicks, SJ, eds, *An Answere vnto Sir Thomas Mores Dialoge* (Washington, DC, forthcoming)

13 John A.R. Dick and James Andrew Clark, eds, *Practice of Prelates* (forthcoming)

14 James Thorpe, *Principles of Textual Criticism* (San Marino 1972) 23

15 John A.R. Dick, ed 'A Critical Edition of William Tyndale's *The Parable of the Wicked Mammon*' (Diss. Yale 1974); cited as *Mammon*

16 This material is drawn mostly from Anthea Hume's annotated bibliography, 'English Protestant Books Printed Abroad, 1525-1535' (CWM 8, 2:1065-91).

17 *An Apology made by George Joy, to satisfy, if it may be, W. Tindale, 1535*, ed. Edward Arber, The English Scholar's Library 13 (London: Unwin Brothers, 1882) 33

18 *A boke made by John Frith ... answeringe vnto M. mores lettur* (Antwerp: H. Peetersen van Middelburch?, 1533?)

19 'Hutchins' may be an alternate family name indicating an inheritance acquired through marriage (Daniell 12).

20 Douglas H. Parker ed (Toronto 1992)

21 The title page of the 1534 Genesis is reproduced in Pentateuch, p. xlv.

22 My comments on problems with the colophons are based on M.E. Kronenberg's article, 'Notes on English Printing in the Low Countries,' *The Library*, 4th Series, 9 (1929) 139-63.

23 John A.R. Dick, 'Political Revisions in Tyndale's *Mammon* and *Prac-*

tice,' in *Church, State & Word,* Proceedings of the William Tyndale Conference, Washington, DC, 14–17 July 1994 (forthcoming)

24 W.W. Greg, 'The Rationale of Copy-Text,' *Studies in Bibliography* 3 (1950) 19–36

25 John A.R. Dick, 'Posthumous Revisions in Tyndale's *Mammon* and *Practice,'* in *Church, State & Word,* Proceedings of William Tyndale Conference, Washington, DC, 14–17 July 1994 (forthcoming)

26 According to the OED, 'wordly' was an alternative spelling for 'worldly' up to the early fifteenth century. Because the form frequently appears in *Mammon, Obedience, Answer,* and *1 John,* the Tyndale editors think it is a deliberate pun.

27 Peter Shillingsburg, 'The Autonomous Author, the Sociology of Texts, and the Polemics of Textual Criticism,' 25 and Steven Mailloux, 'The Rhetorical Politics of Editing' 127 in *Devils and Angels* (see above note 9).

28 Trevor Howard-Hill, 'Variety in Editing and Reading' 47 in *Devils and Angels* (see above note 9).

29 *Textual Scholarship: An Introduction* (New York 1992)

30 Anne M. O'Donnell, SND, 'Erasmus and Tyndale as Biblical Exegetes,' *Erasmus of Rotterdam Yearbook Fifteen* (1995) (forthcoming)

31 Cf. Germain Marc'hadour, *The Bible in Works of Thomas More* 1–5 (Nieuwkoop 1969–72) 3, 194–6. More's other key texts are Ps. 67:7, Matt. 16:18, Matt. 18:20, Matt. 28:20, John 16:13, and John 20:30; cf. *Bible* 4:117.

32 James Thorpe, 'Literary and Historical Editing: The Values and Limits of Diversity,' in *Devils and Angels* (see above note 9); cited as 'Diversity'

33 Stephen J. Mayer ed 'A Critical Edition of *An exposicion vpon the v. vi. vii. chapters of Matthew* by William Tyndale' (Diss Yale, 1975), cited as *Matthew*

34 Alan G.R. Smith, *The Emergence of a Nation State: The Commonwealth of England, 1529–1660* (London 1984), 'Framework of Events 1529–1558,' 3–6

35 In *Christian Humanism and the Reformation,* ed. John C. Olin (New York 1965) 97

5   Editing the Peter Martyr Library

The *Peter Martyr Library*[1] is a series of English translations of the Italian Reformer Pietro Martire Vermigli (1499–1562). It has an initial series of twelve volumes at various stages of preparation, with a further series projected. The first volume, 'Early Writings,' is now available.[2]

First a word about Martyr himself, since he is not so familiar as his contemporaries in the Reformation.[3] Born in Florence in 1499, Pier Mariano Vermigli entered the novitiate at the Lateran Congregation of the Canons Regular of St Augustine in Fiesole, the historic Etruscan town overlooking his native city. He took the name Pietro Martire from a Dominican inquisitor of Verona canonized in 1253. After four years he advanced to the University of Padua, where he spent eight formative years studying philosophy and theology. From his teachers and his own extensive reading – he is one of the most erudite of reformers – he learned to rely most heavily on three names: Aristotle, Aquinas, and Gregory of Rimini.[4] These historic figures directed his steps to Aristotelian philosophy, Thomist theology, and Augustinian spirituality. He also excelled in the public debate featured in university learning, a training ground for his future polemical involvements.

Vermigli advanced rapidly in his Order, as teacher, preacher, and administrator. During his triennium as Abbot of S. Pietro ad Aram in Naples (1537–40), he joined the circle of the Spanish exile Juan de Valdés, which included Bernardino Ochino. Here the Erasmian influence of the Spanish *spirituali* is evident, as is the influence of works by other northern reformers then in underground circulation. His preaching placed him under suspicion of heresy. Being reinstated, he was elected one of the Visitors of the Order, and named Prior of the influential monastery of S. Frediano at Lucca. In just over a year he reformed the manners and morals of both cloister and hearth, and established a teaching faculty of renown. Philip McNair comments: 'S. Frediano became the first and last reformed theological college in pre-Tridentine Italy – a miniature but brilliant university with Martyr as its Rector;' again, 'what he achieved in so short a time is one of the marvels of the Continental Reformation.'[5]

In July 1542 Pope Paul III reestablished the Roman Inquisition. When he was summoned to appear before it, Vermigli made ready to renounce his vows and depart the country. He met up with Bernardino Ochino, and they crossed the border in September 1542. His second career, as reformer, saw him teaching in Strasbourg, Oxford, and Zurich, sponsored in turn by Bucer, Cranmer and Bullinger. He participated in the Oxford Disputation 1549 and the Poissy Colloquy 1561. After two sojourns in Strasbourg, interrupted by five years in Oxford, Martyr found peace in Zurich for the last five years of his life. Heinrich Bullinger had always been his favourite colleague; he shared his confession of faith (the 'Second Helvetic') with Martyr, who died in peace in November 1562.

This brief survey of his life and work suggests the contours of the textual situation facing our translation project. No collected edition of Martyr's works has appeared nor critical editions established. More-over, the popularity of the Commonplace Book reinforced the image of Martyr as chief founder of 'Reformed Scholasticism.' While it is true that he is responsible for casting reformed ideas in Aristotelian categories, his debt to humanism as well as his biblicism qualify the judgment.[6]

Roland Bainton noted: 'Erasmus of Rotterdam has never had his due. The reason is in part that he founded no church to perpetuate his memory.'[7] The name of Peter Martyr could be substituted fairly in that sentence. The two men were separated by almost a generation. When Erasmus published his *New Testament* in 1516, Vermigli was pursuing his monastic vocation in Fiesole. When the great humanist scholar died in 1536, the monk was rising in his Order and was presumably in Rome assisting the reforming Cardinals in preparing the *Consilium ... de emendanda ecclesia* published the following year. The Erasmian influence among that highranking group of churchmen was reinforced when Vermigli served a triennium in Naples. The group of *spirituali* surrounding Juan de Valdés were nurtured by that 'Italian Evangelism' now recognized as a potent and widespread force in Italy before the inquisitorial year 1542. And we know of the strength of Erasmian spirituality in the Valdesian homeland of Spain and in Valdés' own teaching in Naples.

Italian reactions to Erasmus were mixed. After the 1537 *Consilium*, growing opposition to the great Humanist scholar marked the beginnings of the Counter-Reformation.[8] For his part, Vermigli echoed Erasmus' *Ciceronianus* in regarding pagan sources as useful servants but dangerous masters. His is not an intentional *philosophia Christi*, but he would accept the Erasmian standard: 'All Christian speech should have the savour of Christ.'[9]

I now turn to the *Peter Martyr Library* Project. What sparked the modern revival of scholarly interest in a reformer largely neglected for three centuries? Two nineteenth century authors wrote biographies, but almost a century passed until interest in Martyr revived. In 1949 Mariano Di Gangi turned his attention to his countryman in a BD thesis for The Presbyterian College, Montreal.[10] Although I first met Di Gangi that same year, it was Thomas F. Torrance, my Doktorvater at Edinburgh, who introduced me to Vermigli and persuaded me to concentrate on his doctrine of sacrament for my own thesis, accepted in 1953 and published in 1957.[11] Two others were engaged in doctoral studies on Martyr about the same time, Gordon Huelin at the University of London,[12] and Philip McNair at Oxford.[13] The first has not been published, but the second is the definitive biography for the Italian period: *Peter Martyr in Italy: an Anatomy of Apostasy.*

The publication of monographs during the sixties and seventies allowed me to identify a group of interested scholars, leading to an international conference at McGill in 1977. The working title was 'The Cultural Impact of Italian Reformers,' allowing a larger group of Renaissance and Reformation scholars to gather, with Peter Martyr providing the focus; the papers were published in 1980.[14] The presence of the chief Vermigli scholars, among them Robert Kingdon, was an opportunity to deliberate future steps, and to reach agreement on the need for translation. Communication was established through an occasional 'Peter Martyr Newsletter.' A grant for feasibility study was obtained from the American Academy of Religion, enabling us to form an editorial committee and to formulate a proposal for funding and publishing. This was the hardest stage; no major funding for the project itself materialized, although individual editors were more successful. The solution came from Robert Schnucker at the Sixteenth Century Studies Conference. His Society and its press provided the natural habitat for our proposed series of Vermigli translations.

Our translation project is obviously related to the prestigious series *Corpus Reformatorum Italicorum*, which has published selected writings of the Italian 'Reformers,' affectionately known as *eretici* in the trade.

Giorgio Spini is chief editor, working with Cesare Vasoli and John Tedeschi; Aldo Landi is secretary; Emidio Campi is working on the Ochino texts. Vermigli may still have a place in the series but at present there is no firm commitment. This is unfortunate, since the publication of critical texts would greatly aid our translators by providing solid bases for their work.

The canon of writings to which the *Peter Martyr Library* is committed is limited. During Vermigli's twenty years as reformer, six major works and two shorter were published; the first was in Italian, the rest in Latin. His peripatetic lifestyle, combined with his diffidence in preparing clean copy, hindered the publication of his lectures. After his death in 1562 six more books were published, five between 1563 and 1576, and one in 1629. Of these fourteen volumes eight are commentaries: five on the Old Testament, two on the New Testament; and one on Aristotle's Nicomachean Ethics. Three are polemical: one on monastic vows against Richard Smith, his Catholic predecessor at Oxford; another on the two natures of Christ against the Lutheran Johannes Brenz; and the third on the Eucharist, against Stephen Gardiner, the old opponent of both Cranmer and Martyr. The rest include a book of prayers on the Psalms, a commentary on the Apostles' Creed, and the 1549 Oxford Treatise and Disputation on the Eucharist. Minor works, gathered chiefly in the Commonplace books, make up perhaps another large volume. The huge *Loci Communes* was published in London (John Kyngston) in 1576 by Robert Masson, minister of the French church in London, reprinted by Froschauer of Zurich in 1580. This was expanded into a three-volume work by Pietro Perna of Basel (1580–82) by including numerous minor works. Translated as *The Common Places of Peter Martyr* by Anthony Marten (London: Denham & Middleton, 1583) and dedicated to Queen Elizabeth, the *loci* became a favourite resource for generations of Reformed clergy, notably Puritans in Britain and America. The circulation of his works is still a matter of research, particularly by Marvin Anderson, who has recently traced copies in Eastern Europe.[15]

Martyr was fortunate in his publishers. Christopher Froschauer was his own favourite; his offices were within walking distance of Martyr's Zurich residence. The first of the eight works published during his lifetime begin with the 1542 *Credo* (Basel, no publisher named), followed by the Oxford *Treatise on the Sacraments* (London: Wolfe). After that Froschauer of Zurich published four and Pietro Perna of Basel two. Of the posthumous works, Froschauer published five, and Perna the 3-volume set of *Loci*. The *Loci* enjoyed wide circulation and several reprints in the next century, including a further Zurich edition, one each in Heidelberg and London, and four by Aubert of Geneva in the seventeenth century (1623, 1624, 1626, 1627). Martyr himself edited only half of his published works. Of the lecture series in Strasbourg only the Aristotle and Judges were published, the latter edited by John Jewel who had heard the lectures while living with Martyr in Strasbourg during the Marian exile. The Zurich series on Samuel and Kings were edited by others. Fortunately the *Loci* include a representative selection of the many scholia with which Martyr laced his commentaries. The length of the scholia ranges from a page to treatises of fifty pages and more. Just two of them, for instance, on Justification and Predestination, will comprise one of our volumes.

Thus we have a short list of extant titles, with first editions readily available. Most works will make books of from 250 to 500 pages, although some are much longer because of the numerous scholia. Should we emulate the commonplace practice of offering a variety of scholia? One volume of 'Philosophical Writings' will do this, besides the two treatises just mentioned. It has not been decided whether to include Martyr's reply to Gardiner – 800 quarto pages of largely patristic quotations – in the *Library*.

In preparing the initial volumes for publication we faced a number of procedural and organizational problems. The beginning of every multi-volume project involves the logistical work of organizing a team for translating and editing. This requires an efficient means of communication, by newsletter or computer network, as well as considerable effort in developing a realistic timetable in conjunction with the Press. In the case of the *Peter Martyr Library*, we are fortunate in having as publishers an organization already part of our interest group, as it were, namely the Sixteenth Century Studies Conference. Their *Sixteenth Century Journal Publications, Inc.* has as chief functionaries Robert V. Schnucker and Paula Presley, both of whom are members of our Editorial Committee, one serving as Managing Editor, and the other as Copy Editor.

A second major task is that of identifying reliable texts for translation. Normally this means first editions, collated with later ones. This has been made easier for us by the pioneer bibliographical work of Professors Donnelly and Kingdon, published in 1990.[16] Ideally, scholarly work on Martyr should begin with producing critical editions. Professor Donnelly has done this for the *Dialogus* on christology, which he has translated as Volume 2 of the *Library*. Otherwise we expect translators to perform the sometimes onerous task of collation. Fortunately the corpus of Vermigli's work has been gathered in Zurich's Zentralbibliothek, and is available in microform.[17] Thus we have first editions, microfilm and microfiche for all our texts. So far we have not discovered any unpublished material, such as the missing lecture series from the first Strasbourg series.

The task of developing a stylesheet has also proved relatively simple, since our publishers' policy, for its Journal as well as monographs and series, is to follow the *Chicago Manual of Style* closely. After examining similar stylesheets – including the 20-page document for the CWE – we are obviously delighted that decisions in this area, including preparing indices, are in the capable hands of our copy editor.

Format was another area that required deliberation. We have decided to render annotations as footnotes for ease of reading and to place commentaries in the introductions. Annotation presents difficulties because Vermigli displays the sixteenth-century cavalier attitude in citing sources. He relies a great deal on memory and paraphrase, evidencing the breadth of his reading in classical, biblical, and patristic literature. Tracing patristic quotations, especially from Martyr's favourite, Augustine, is a formidable task. Even more elusive are his citations from the classical Greek author Galen.

Translation poses another dilemma since it must be both faithful to the text and representative of contemporary style. Once the accuracy of the translation is verified by our Latinist, we expect individual editors, in collaboration with the General Editors, to ensure a certain uniformity without abandoning the dynamic qualities proper to the text at hand. Martyr's own Latin style is good but verbose, often pedantic, and sometimes downright baffling. It does not compare with Erasmus' 'proud Latinity,' as Johann Huizinga calls it. In the interest of readability we have taken the liberty of breaking up long sentences, of introducing paragraphs, and adding headings. Usually we indicate the original pagination in square brackets and include the original section numbering to accommodate scholarly readers. These measures are designed to make the modern text more accessible.

My co-editor Patrick Donnelly has called my attention to a distinction made by William C. Creasy, the translator of Thomas à Kempis. He uses the term 'stencil translation' to denote the work of the translator who 'moves almost as a copyist, working through the text phrase by phrase.' This produces a literal but stilted, even confusing, rendering of the original. Creasy contrasts this method with another he calls 'aureate translation.' Here the translator uses the sentence as the basic unit, 'feeling free to embellish and expand it.'[18] We all know how tempting is the first method, resulting in a Latinate translation, and how difficult is the second. It goes without saying that the 'aureate translation' remains the goal.

Chief Works of Peter Martyr Vermigli

Note: These works are listed in the order of their first editions.

1544 *Una Simplice Dichiaratione sopra gli xii articoli della fede christiana* Basel, N.P.

1549 *Tractatio de sacramento eucharistiae, habita in universitate Oxoniense. Ad hec: Disputatio habita MD XLIX.* London: [R. Wolfe]

1551 *In Selectissimam S. Pauli Priorem ad Corinthios Epistolam ... Commentarii ...* Zurich: C. Froschoverus

1558 *In Epistolam S. Pauli Apostoli ad Romanos ... Commentarii ...* Basel: P. Perna

1559 *Defensio Doctrinae Veteris et Apostolicae de Sacrosancto Eucharistiae Sacramento ...* Zurich: Froschoverus

1559 *Defensio ... de Caelibatu Sacerdotum & Votis monasticis.* Basel: P. Perna

1561 *In Librum Iudicum ... Commentarii ...* Zurich: C. Froschoverus

1561 *Dialogus de Utraque in Christo Natura ...* Zurich: C. Froschoverus

1563 *In Primum, Secundum, et Initium Tertii Libri Ethicorum Aristotelis ad Nicomachum ...* Zurich: C. Froschoverus

1564 *Preces Sacrae ex Psalmis Davidis Desumptae ...* Zurich: C. Froschoverus

1564 *In Duos Libros Samuelis Prophetae ... Commentarii ...* Zurich: C. Froschoverus

1566 *Melachim Id Est, Regum Libri Duo Posteriores cum Commentariis.* Zurich: C. Froschoverus

1569 *In Primum Librum Mosis Qui Vulgo Genesis Dicitur Commentarii ...* Zurich: C. Froschoverus

1629 *In Lamentationes Sanctissimi Ieremiae Prophetae ... Commentarium.* Zurich: J.J. Bodmer

NOTES

1 *The Peter Martyr Library* is published by Thomas Jefferson University Press and Sixteenth Century Journal Publishers, Inc. General Editors are J.P. Donnelly, SJ, Marquette University and J.C. McLelland, McGill University. Editorial Committee: Marvin W. Anderson (Southern Bap-

tist Theological Seminary, Lousville KY), Rita Belladonna (York University), Edward J. Furcha (McGill University), Frank A. James III (Reformed Theological Seminary, Maitland FL), William J. Klempa (The Presbyterian College, Montreal). Managing Editor: Robert V. Schnucker, Sixteenth Century Journal, Kirksville MO.

2 *Early Writings,* Peter Martyr Library Volume One, edited with introductions and notes by J.C. McLelland. pp viii + 230. Includes Biographical Introduction (Philip M.J. McNair); Apostles' Creed and Schism (Mariano Di Gangi); Theses for Debate (J.C. McLelland).

3 The definitive biography for the Italian period is that of Philip M.J. McNair, *Peter Martyr in Italy: An Anatomy of Apostasy* (Oxford 1967). See also his 'Biographical Introduction' to Volume 1 of the *Peter Martyr Library* (previous note).

4 See J. Simler, Martyr's first biographer, *Life of Martyr,* E.T. in Duffield and McLelland, *The Life, Early Letters & Eucharistic Writings of Peter Martyr* (Abingdon 1989) 35–7; McNair, *Peter Martyr in Italy* 86–115; Frank A. James III, 'A Late Medieval Augustinian Parallel in Reformation Thought: *Gemina Praedestinatio* in Gregory of Rimini and Peter Martyr Vermigli' in H. Oberman ed, *Via Augustini: the Recovery of Augustine in the Later Middle Ages, Renaissance and Reformation* (Leiden 1993) 157–88.

5 McNair, *Peter Martyr in Italy,* 216, 221. For Valdés, Ochino and Erasmian influences cf *ibidem* 25–6, 35–6.

6 See Brian G. Armstrong, *Calvinism and the Amyraut Heresy* (Madison 1969); cf J.P. Donnelly, *Calvinism and Scholasticism in Vermigli's Doctrine of Man and Grace* (Leiden 1976) 197ff, and J.C. McLelland, 'Peter Martyr Vermigli: Scholastic or Humanist?' in McLelland ed, *Peter Martyr Vermigli and Italian Reform* 141–51.

7 R. Bainton, *Erasmus of Christendom* (New York 1969) vii

8 See Myron P. Gilmore, 'Italian Reactions to Erasmian Humanism' in H.A. Oberman ed, *Itinerarium Italicum* (Leiden 1975) 61–115.

9 CWE 28, ed A.H.T.Levi (Toronto 1986) 388, 439

10 See M. Di Gangi, *Peter Martyr Vermigli, Renaissance Man, Reformation Master* (Lanham 1993).

11 *The Visible Words of God: the Sacramental Theology of Peter Martyr Vermigli* (Edinburgh 1957; Grand Rapids 1961)

12 'Peter Martyr and the English Reformation,' PhD dissertation, University of London 1955; unpublished

13 See above note 3.

14 *Peter Martyr Vermigli and Italian Reform,* ed J.C. McLelland (Waterloo 1980) viii, 155; ten chapters by P.F. Grendler, C. Vasoli, R. Belladonna,

A. Santosuosso, A. D'Andrea, M.W. Anderson, P.M.J. McNair, J.P. Donnelly, R.M. Kingdon and J.C. McLelland.

15 M.W. Anderson, *Peter Martyr: a Reformer in Exile (1542–1562): A Chronology of Biblical Writings in England and Europe* (Nieuwkoop 1975); the Register (467–86) is expanded in J.P. Donnelly's 1990 *Bibliography* (see note 16) 155–97, Register Epistolarum Vermilii.

16 *A Bibliography of the Works of Peter Martyr Vermigli* (Kirksville 1980), compiled by John Patrick Donnelly, SJ in collaboration with Robert M. Kingdon, with a Register of Vermigli's Correspondence by Marvin W. Anderson

17 *Inter Documentation Company*, Leiden – 'Reformed Protestantism' series. Cf Donnelly, *Bibliography*, xii–xiv for details of library holdings.

18 *The Imitation of Christ: A New Reading of the 1441 Latin Autograph Manuscript* by Wm. C. Creasy (Macon 1989) xxiv–xxv.

6 Erasmus in Amsterdam and Toronto

In a conference on editing texts from the age of Erasmus it seems appropriate to say something about editing the works of Erasmus himself. Remarkably, at this time two comprehensive series are proceeding together, the new critical edition from Amsterdam (ASD) and the *Collected Works of Erasmus* from University of Toronto Press (CWE). When I was asked to participate in this gathering it seemed to me that I could most usefully contribute from the perspective of personal experience with both of these, experience which – apart from the annotation of two volumes of the correspondence series in CWE – has been to date largely organizational and supervisory, as chairman of the Editorial Board of CWE, and as member of the Council responsible for the direction of the new *Opera omnia*.

A paper from an unexpected source set in motion the reflections which will follow. In October 1991 a conference was held at Chantilly on patristic and late antique studies in Germany and France between the years 1870 and 1930. One of the participants was a scholar at the University of British Columbia, Dr Mark Vessey, and the title of his paper was, 'After the Maurists: the Oxford Correspondence of Dom Germain Morin, O.S.B.'[1] Dom Germain, a patristics scholar of stature, was chosen by Dr Vessey to exemplify, 'the variety of relations that may hold between the careers and activities of individual scholars and the institutions of academic life.' This is a theme of some urgent interest to all of us, and of particular concern to the collective scholarship required for the editing of extensive series of texts.

Dom Germain is an instructive figure, and his career speaks to us. He was a monk of the well-known Benedictine abbey of Maredsous, and his scholarly career was the subject of a monograph published in the Instrumenta Patristica in 1986.[2] Although his religious calling might seem to be rather obviously suited to a vocation in the tradition of the Maurists, Dom Germain was in fact a highly unconventional – and unconventual – figure whose life is oddly reminiscent of that led by another Benedictine scholar of the present century, Dom David Knowles. He was born in Caen in Normandy in 1861, and he made his monastic profession at Maredsous in 1882. Although his evident aptitude for textual scholarship was strongly encouraged by his superiors, the very nature of his investigations – initially a critical edition of the works of Caesarius, the sixth-century bishop of Arles – took him repeatedly outside the precincts of Maredsous to Brussels, Munich, and Paris, and over the following three decades to most of the great libraries of Europe. It was in England, however, that he found a tradition and community of scholarship which seemed to him an authentic continuation of the work of the Bollandists and Maurists whose lasting accomplishments had been the inspiration of his life. His friendship and scholarly communion with two Oxford scholars in particular – Cuthbert Turner and a Scot, Alexander Souter – gave rise to a correspondence over three decades which was preserved in the Bodleian Library, and which furnished the evidence for Dr Vessey's examination of Morin's career.

Vessey used the Oxford materials not simply to add some details to the existing monograph on Morin but more importantly, to explore the significance of Dom Germain's career for the history of textual scholarship as such. Unlike David Knowles, Morin remained on good terms with his monastery and his abbot, but each year he spent several months away from the cloister in search not only of manuscripts but also of scholarly fellowship and support. When he first set out on his investigations, his abbot urged him to do just that, to seek out 'le commerce des hommes experimentés' whose good advice would supply anything that he lacked in his scholarly formation.[3]

Apart from Léopold Delisle and Louis Duchesne he seems to have found French scholars and scholarship disappointing. Eventually he found a scholarly home in the monastery of Sankt Bonifaz in Munich, and in the course of a long life – he died in 1946 – he lived from time to time in Oxford, London, Cambridge, in Einsiedeln, in Strasbourg, in Paris, Leuven, and Milan, always seeking (with the full approval of his abbot) an 'atelier d'érudition' not too far from Maredsous and in close proximity to a serious library.[4] Throughout that time it was to England, particularly to Oxford, that he was drawn as his intellectual home. It is clear that he romanticized his fantasy fatherland, but his sense that it was in England that Christian textual scholarship survived in the great traditions of the past was absolute. In 1905 he was awarded the degree of D.Litt *honoris causa* at Oxford. I quote Mark Vessey on the meaning of this recognition for the recipient: 'For Morin the ceremony retained its full social and quasi-religious importance. He had been received into a society, a brotherhood, a family of scholars. No other moment of association, with the single exception of his entry into the monastery, would ever count for as much with him as the day on which the Oxfordmen clothed him in their academic garb, pronounced their solemn formulas, and admitted him to their ranks.'[5]

In the career of Dom Germain Morin Vessey sees an illustrative commentary on the sociology of modern textual scholarship and Christian philology. The vision of the great Benedictine enterprise at St Maur, the legacy of Mabillon and of the scholarly association at Saint-Germain-des-Prés has been cherished by generations of scholars ever since the upheavals of the French Revolution razed their institutional and spiritual foundations. The Benedictine Order itself responded in a revival of scholarship to which the *Révue Bénédictine*, newly established at the turn of the century, bears witness. But (as Vessey points out), the inherent tension between the Benedictine rule of *stabilitas* and the demands of research cannot be ignored, and David Knowles observed in his essay on the Maurist Congregation that the original enterprise itself can be seen to have depended for its illustrious achievement on the temporary conjunction of a set of favourable circumstances.[6]

One might add that the revival of monastic life in the years after World War I was accompanied by a tightening of coenobitic discipline in general, so that periods of extended ex-claustration for the individual monk even for the most commendable scholarly needs were viewed without enthusiasm – as Knowles himself was to learn. Morin was not the first, nor would he be the last to fancy that in the collegiate societies of Oxford and Cambridge a secular continuation of pre-Revolutionary scholarly and Christian ideals perdured in a country that has never known a revolution. As Vessey recalls, long before the time of Morin the comparison was not lost upon Edward Gibbon when he penned his immortal ironies about the somnolent fellows of his Oxford college:

> The shelves of their library groan under the weight of the Benedictine folios, of the editions of the fathers, and the collections of the Middle Ages, which have issued from the single abbey of St. Germain de Prés at Paris. A composition of genius must be the offspring of one mind;

but such works of industry, as may be divided among many hands, and must be continued during many years, are the peculiar province of a laborious community. If I inquire into the manufactures of the monks of Magdalen, if I extend the enquiry to the other colleges of Oxford and Cambridge, a silent blush or a scornful frown will be the only reply.[7]

Gibbon's comment points to another aspect of the great enterprises of the Maurists and Bollandists: the possibility there offered of transmitting to the new talent of a younger generation the intellectual zeal and exacting disciplines required for textual scholarship. While Morin deplored his failures to attract younger pupils to his personal *atelier* to carry on his work, his English colleagues fared no better. Whatever advantages the collegiate societies of Oxford and Cambridge may have offered to scholarly communion, they did nothing to alter the haphazard emergence of potential scholarly successors. Dom Germain's Oxford friend, Cuthbert Hamilton Turner, a fellow of Gibbon's old college and the first editor of the *Journal of Theological Studies* (founded in 1900) wrote in 1928 to an associate, 'My undergraduate friends did splendidly in Greats, five of them getting firsts. There is one of them, ... a junior fellow of Balliol, whom I must make you acquainted with when you next come to Oxford. [He] is Roger Mynors, whose research work is on the Carolingian revival, and he is editing Cassiodorus *de inst. div. litt.* and *saec. litt.*'[8]

While no one could complain at the fate which gave him Roger Mynors as a promising pupil, Turner's personal interests lay in early Christian philology, and he edited the earliest surviving texts of occidental canon law. Mynors, as the world knows, came to divide his formidable talents between literary texts of classical antiquity and those of the middle ages, not to mention Erasmus. While his erudition and intellectual sympathies betrayed the influence of such as Cuthbert Hamilton Turner, he was in no sense a successor in the older man's field.

The truth is, surely, that the demands of modern textual scholarship are such that no one society, however much enamoured of the ideals of coenobitic erudition, and however well-supplied it may be with resources human and institutional, can expect to re-enact the achievements of the past in the same fashion. What is more, the development of an academic *profession* in the nineteenth and early twentieth centuries was dominated by German and American models, and created an entirely new context for serious scholarly research, one that emphasized enormously the role of the university over that of the eighteenth century academy and its analogous societies of private and independent scholarship.

In my own lifetime I have witnessed in England the failure of a Benedictine attempt to re-enact the past. Quarr Abbey on the Isle of Wight was founded as a place of exile for the monastery of Solesmes at the time of the French anti-clerical legislation in the first years of this century. When Solesmes was allowed to return to its historic home, the French Benedictines left behind a small community to form the nucleus of an English house in their own Congregation. A part of their legacy was the liturgical scholarship of the Solesmes tradition, and for a time it seemed that this might take root at Quarr. As a student in Oxford I well remember the picturesque sight of Dom Hugh Farmer working in the Duke Humfrey Library in Benedictine habit and cowl to the common delight of the medievalists around him and the edification of the staff. In retrospect it seems that I should have recognized Dom Hugh's vigils in Bodley as the foreshadowing of what was soon to come. Today, as a professor of medieval history at the University of Reading he retains the erudition but has dropped the cowl. Another such was Dom Paul Meyvaert, also a monk of Quarr and today, one of the best-known (lay) medievalists in the world. It is also true that the first scholar I can recall to comment on this evolution of Quarr Abbey – and with regret – was Sir Roger Mynors.

It is also pertinent to remark that my own career has been shared between two societies dedicated entirely to scholarly research as their main reason for existence. All Souls is surely the one college at either Oxford or Cambridge where corporate scholarship from generation unto generation might be a serious possibility. There is no trace of it now or (to the best of my knowledge) has there been at any time in the past. Interests are shared, most certainly, but collaboration rarely extends beyond the occasional joint seminar. At the Pontifical Institute of Mediaeval Studies (PIMS) the common focus on the middle ages would seem to bring the possibility even nearer, and perhaps the publication of such series as *Medieval Studies* and 'Studies and Texts' might be thought actually to exemplify it. These draw routinely upon the energies and erudition of the entire community at PIMS, and it is difficult to imagine such enterprises continuing without the routine collaboration of scholars there. Beyond that however, while there is much exchange of learning and there are many shared concerns, each fellow tends to pursue her or his own path. The various series published by the Pontifical Institute represent a kind of collaborative scholarship which would doubtless be much more difficult in a less intimate society, but it is not the kind of thing envisaged by Dom Germain when, in 1890, he wrote to his abbot with the youthful idea of establishing a 'petit Saint-Germain' at Maredsous. As for the recruitment of younger scholars, this too occurs as elsewhere in an unpredictable and haphazard fashion.

This is the background against which I would like to shape my reflections upon the two editions of Erasmus which have come into existence in the last three decades or so. Apart from obvious questions about differing aims and objectives – the establishment of text, mechanisms of control and the like – important as these practical issues are, the Erasmus enterprise of our time is in itself an interesting moment in intellectual history and in the history of scholarship. Both editions are unmistakably the work of a 'laborious community' in Gibbon's sense. Indeed, it is probable that at this moment there is more scholarly energy and time being expended on the editing of Erasmus than on any other historical author. I estimate that the new critical edition, ASD, has engaged the efforts of some seventy scholars to date, and it is no more than half-way to completion even if – what seems altogether likely – the correspondence is never included in ASD. For the *Collected Works of Erasmus* (CWE), the current directory of those involved extends to one hundred and eighty-four names, among whom I number eighty-eight who are presently involved in translation, annotation, editorial supervision, or in an advisory capacity. All told, it would be fair to say that, since their inception, these two projects have drawn directly upon the assistance of more than two hundred scholars internationally. And the international aspect is another that deserves notice. The countries under contribution to both ASD and CWE include – apart from Canada and the United States – England and Scotland in the United Kingdom, France, Germany, Italy, Austria, Switzerland, Belgium, The Netherlands, Spain, and Australia.

There are two general issues which seem to me to be raised by the simultaneous appearance of these ambitious series. Contemporary criticism reminds us that every new edition participates in the continuing life of a text, and that the editors indeed participate in the text itself through what they bring to it. Accordingly, it is important that we become aware of the context of our own work, even as we attempt to discover the context of the original authorship. Where, then, does the present international enterprise stand in the history of editing itself? And secondly, why does Erasmus emerge in our own time as such a dominant figure?

Both the Amsterdam *Opera omnia* and the *Collected Works of Erasmus* are in a tradition which grew up after the French Revolution with the emergence of the modern state-supported university, modern learned academies, and – not of least importance – the modern nation state. The willingness of governments to encourage and, to a degree, to finance such bodies is as much a part of the apparatus of the democratic nation state as is the standing army, although the two are rarely linked in the same sentence. Both ASD and CWE were launched with the prospect of such subsidy, direct or indirect, and the Dutch edition still receives it. That benefit reflects the prestige of the long tradition of Dutch scholarship, and most certainly Dutch pride in a most famous if largely non-resident son. In Canada, it is reasonable to see the launching of CWE too as an expression of post-war national confidence and pride, as a late product of the impulse that led to the setting-up of the Massey Commission in the 1950s, and of the government's acceptance that, in a country where old wealth and richly-endowed foundations scarcely existed, it had a role to play in the support not only of science and technology, but also of the arts and humanities.

In addition to these similarities in their origins both ASD and CWE, like other such projects, have been organized to respond to the individualism of intellectual life in the largely secularist and positivistic atmosphere that has prevailed in the West since 1815. Both rely on the international community of universities for recruitment, as both rely increasingly on developments in technology to nourish a sense of association between the scattered individuals involved. At the same time, both have recognized the need for a nucleus of scholars and directors to co-ordinate the enterprise and be answerable to funding authorities. Both have an editorial board, an executive body within the board, and a large circle of appointed scholar-advisors. Both – which is not without special interest – were favoured from the outset by the staunch and indispensable support of a learned Press, something that any student of sixteenth-century Europe will recognize as a gift from the past. Perhaps the most notable development of these two independent but parallel series is the fact that, with quite distinct origins, they have now come to a state of close and easy collaboration, including the recruitment of scholars one from another and, most recently, a strategic grant from the by no means affluent Council of ASD to help finance a critical piece of research for CWE which lacked itself the funds to pay for it. There indeed is testimony of scholarly concord and fraternity, if testimony were wanting.

What of their aims and objectives? That of ASD is to establish a modern, critical edition of the original text in succession to the first from Basel of 1538–40, and to the second from Leiden a century and a half later. As an authorized edition, that of Basel followed the *Ordines* of Erasmus' personal arrangement of his works, its chief accomplishment and aim being to establish the canon of his writings. This would help to protect his reputation against the many forgeries circulated over his name during his lifetime, an activity that might be expected to continue after his death. The only significant deviation from the canon was the omission, no doubt for commercial reasons, of Erasmus' editions and translations of patristic and classical texts.

The Leiden edition, whose ten folio volumes appeared between 1703 and 1707, was prompted in the first place by the growing scarcity of that from Basel. It was initiated by a bookseller of Leiden, Petrus vander Aa, who commissioned Jean Leclerc to supervise the publication of a new edition. Leclerc – Joannes Clericus – was a liberal minded scholar of Huguenot ancestry who, as a theological student, had adopted the views of the Dutch Arminians and fled from the Calvinism of Geneva to serve the Remonstrant cause in Amsterdam. While the new edition was not without its problems, substantial advances were made. The complete commentary by Gerardus Listrius was added to the *Praise of Folly*. Likewise, Clericus included at the end of the *Colloquies* the 'Conflictus Thaliae et Barbariae' which had been printed for the first time in 1693. The most substantial addition to the *corpus Erasmianum* was in the correspondence, which was considerably enlarged from posthumous editions and from the last-minute discovery of the Deventer letter-book. Moreover, the Leiden edition was the first to attempt a chronological arrangement of the letters. In the presentation of the New Testament the *Annotations*, hitherto printed separately, were printed at the foot of the columns of text, where they were both a convenience and a source of confusion to later users. The Leiden edition was not flawless. Some footnotes were added by several hands in a haphazard fashion, and there were other shortcomings.[9] One of its most helpful contributions to successive generations of scholars was one that is rarely mentioned – the *Index vocabulorum et locorum* which, if it was not done perfectly, was an astonishing thing to have done at all.

About the circumstances which led to the undertaking of ASD I shall say more, but it seems appropriate here to cite the tribute paid by its initiators to their predecessor: 'Even after they will eventually have been superseded ..., Clericus' eleven folios, well-produced and beautifully adorned, will always stand as a monument in which 18th-century civilization expressed its indebtedness to one of its great teachers.'

While the Amsterdam edition was logically intended to bring to Erasmus' *corpus* all of the resources of modern textual scholarship, the objectives of CWE were quite different. In order to propagate the works of Erasmus to what he would have viewed as an illiterate age, it was decided to produce a 'Collected' edition in English. The Englishing of Erasmus' vast output is a work of double jeopardy. Initially, it was necessary to devise procedures to establish a base text where none from ASD was available, and this could only be done from collation of successive editions. It was decided, in contrast to the traditional editorial practice which governed ASD, to make the fullest text published during Erasmus' lifetime the base text of the translation. It may be said that in practice, with the exception of a few major literary works such as the *Adagia*, the complexity of this task has been far less than was originally anticipated. There is an obvious difference in annotation. Philological issues are rarely of interest to CWE, except in the *Annotations* to the New Testament. Notes on historical references are much fuller; notes on sources are roughly the same. With a working text in Latin established, there remains a large issue of the English rendering which must be accurate, yet accessible and written in a style that will last while still responding to the nuances, shifting moods, and rhetorical variations of the original. ASD is spared all of that. Another of the most important and least obvious problems of CWE, unknown to the *Opera omnia*, is the need to contain the scale of annotation yet at the same time, provide enough information drawn from current scholarship to illuminate and elucidate the text.

In scope, the two series are more alike than might at first be thought probable. Neither will reproduce Erasmus' editions of the Fathers or of classical texts; both follow Erasmus' original arrangement, ASD more closely than CWE. Otherwise, for the most part texts found in one will be found in the other. There are however some significant differences. ASD will publish the *scholia* on the *Vita Hieronymi* where CWE will not. Unlike CWE, ASD must edit Erasmus' edition of the New Testament, a task so complex that it led the Council to agree that here, at least, CWE's policy of printing the final version as the base text was indispensable. ASD, on the other hand, does not intend to re-edit P.S. Allen's monumental *Opus epistolarum*, while the translation and extensive re-annotation of the correspondence has been a feature of CWE from the beginning, and is likely to constitute the needed updating of Erasmus' correspondence at least for our time.

What we see then in these two vast undertakings is a new kind of *'atelier d'érudition'* where faxes, internet, and regular gatherings at international conferences have supplanted the cloistered association and *stabilitas* of the Maurist Congregation. For all of the differences, it must be said that it is precisely this change in the sociology of scholarship that has permitted the extension and elaboration of that earlier enterprise into our own time. It should also be admitted that the need for many scattered, industrious teams to assemble and elucidate the achievement of a single individual is a vivid commentary on the history of erudition. It recalls to my mind at least, the apocalyptic citation from the Book of Daniel which so strangely adorns the marble tablet at the entrance to the Bodleian Library: 'Plurimi pertransibunt et multiplex erit scientia' ('Many shall pass over, and knowledge shall be manifold' Dan 12:4). It would be entertaining, if not alarming, to have Erasmus' reflections on that.

With this said about the nature of these editions and their place in the history of editorial scholarship there remains the important and perhaps more difficult question: why Erasmus? Some might think it inevitable that sooner or later, a new critical edition of the works would be undertaken, but the resources demanded are enormous, and 'inevitable' has no publication schedule. Nor do I think that these projects could have been foreseen in any very obvious way from the developments either in philological or Reformation studies, where the contributions of Erasmus had long ago been placed satisfactorily on the sidelines. On the contrary, I have the strong impression that the now widespread acceptance of the need to re-assess the place of Erasmus in European intellectual and religious history has come about largely after the fact, once ASD and CWE had begun to appear. The true impetus came very largely, I believe, from a convergence of circumstances, some of which took place far from the groves of academe.

No general explanation can overlook the critical role of individuals, as the history of this question testifies. The first of these, without question, was Percy Stafford Allen, the Oxford classicist whose masterly edition of Erasmus' correspondence provided the initial impetus to his scholarly revival. Allen's devotion to his task leads directly to the traditions of Oxford's Christian philology where we began with the experience of Dom Germain Morin in the very years that Allen was at work. More particularly, the story began at Corpus Christi College, famous for its classical traditions and for the Erasmian principles of its foundation. There Allen was encouraged to compete for the Chancellor's English Essay Prize in a year when the subject set was Erasmus. His widow wrote, 'As he worked he realized that here lay the task for which he had been searching – to edit a new edition of the Letters of Erasmus.'[10] He was encouraged by James Anthony Froude, who held the Regius Chair of Modern History at Oxford. In his Preface to the first volume of the *Opus Epistolarum* Allen wrote, 'It has occupied my leisure for the last thirteen years, and has been carried on under the gloom of Indian summers and in high valleys of Kashmir.'[11] He continued his self-appointed labours with amazing tenacity to the day of his death in 1933. The enormous task of assembling surviving manuscript from hundreds of fugitive repositories, many of them dislocated by World War I, and then of editing the collection in the Leiden edition, redating the letters and identifying recipients, authors, events, and individuals mentioned in the texts, was a single-handed undertaking which now staggers the imagination.

As the first volumes of the *Erasmi Epistolae* began to appear there was an immediate response from France, led by Augustin Renaudet. French historical traditions were attuned to intellectual history where those in England were not; French religious tradition – Gallican and sceptical – was neither Protestant nor ultramontane, and Renaudet famously hailed Erasmus as the prophet of the 'third Church.' The English characteristically were slower to respond, and the first notable English scholar in the field was trained in France as a pupil of Renaudet: a graduate of Somerville College, Oxford, her maiden name was Margaret Mann. The Second World War intervened before the edition was fully published,[12] and it was not until 1958 that the Index volume appeared.

If the catastrophe of World War II seemed to overturn all that the humanist tradition represented, I also believe that it played an essential part in this story. In preparing the background for this paper I have become convinced that a strong impetus behind the emergence of the new *Opera omnia* was the passionate rejection of nationalism which, in the same years, brought into existence the Coal and Steel Community and the Benelux union, and which is still a powerful current in precisely those countries – Belgium, The Netherlands, Luxembourg, France, and Germany – which saw the worst destruction of the war and which now form the nucleus of the European Union.

The official story of the inception of ASD is told in the General Introduction to the first volume.[13] It is signed with four names: J.H. Waszink, Léon-E. Halkin, C. Reedijk, and C.M. Bruehl. They are the key players in the unofficial history of the new edition. Prof. dr. J.H. Waszink, now dead, was the eldest of the four. As a professor at Leiden in the Faculty of Letters he was the promoter of the thesis of

Cornelis Reedijk, and – as will be seen – at one point played an important part in bringing the nascent proposal for a new edition to the attention of the Royal Dutch Academy. His doctoral pupil, Reedijk, was the prime mover and has the best claim to be the initiator of ASD.

Cornelis Reedijk was born on 1 April 1921 in Rotterdam, where from 1933 to 1939 he was a pupil at the Gymnasium Erasmianum. From the age of six he had been a friend of the twin brothers, Alfred and Ernst Kossmann. Alfred was to become a novelist, Ernst a professor of Dutch history at the University of London. In 1939, at the age of eighteen, Reedijk enroled in the Faculty of Letters at Leiden as a student of classics. When the university was closed by the German authorities on 26 November 1940 in response to a violent protest against their dismissal of a Jewish professor, he moved to the University of Amsterdam where in 1942, he qualified for the baccalaureat in classical philology. After that he abandoned formal study and taught himself for the remainder of the war. He was recruited by the father of his close friend, Dr K.F.H. Kossmann, Keeper of the Gemeentebibliotheek – the Municipal Library – of Rotterdam, to collaborate in a project to make Dutch translations of neo-Latin texts. Kossmann suggested that Reedijk translate some of Erasmus' longer poems, which he did before the project was abandoned. After the war he worked as Kossmann's assistant and when his first thesis choice did not work out, he turned to editing the poems of Erasmus. In 1956 he took his doctorate from the University of Leiden under the supervision of Waszink, and the thesis, *The Poems of Desiderius Erasmus*, won high praise. Waszink told Reedijk of a congress on humanism held in Italy in the Tyrol, sponsored by the Catholic University of Milan. This was in the autumn of the same year, 1956. Reedijk addressed the topic of a new, critical edition of the works of Erasmus.

The project of a new critical edition was first mooted, however, not in Holland but in Germany. In the Stellingen[14] issued at his doctoral examination, Reedijk had placed first in a series of thirteen, a citation from K.A. Meissinger's *Erasmus von Rotterdam* published in Vienna in 1942. There, Meissinger had provided a brief outline of such a plan. In 1946 a new Institut für Reformationsforschung was founded at Munich and the first president was Dr K.A. Meissinger. In 1948 the Institut announced its intention of publishing a critical edition of Erasmus' works, 'long overdue after the Leiden edition.' The editorial work was to be entrusted not to a single person but to a team of scholars working 'unter straffer Oberleitung.'[15] In the event, the Munich project could not be carried out but, as we have seen, the incentive had been transferred to Erasmus' native city. It is clear that Meissinger was responding to Allen's edition, and to the reconstruction of Erasmus' life and works to be found there. To quote the words of Cornelis Reedijk about the Dutch edition, 'It is no exaggeration to maintain that the *Opus Epistolarum* is the key to the *Opera Omnia*.'[16]

It is interesting that this wartime initiative had come from the Catholic south of Hitler's Germany. One of the currents that contributed strongly to the revival of interest in Erasmus was the changing relationship between the Christian confessions in western Europe, notably in France and Germany. Conversations between Protestant and Catholic leaders which had begun before the war were resumed after 1945, and Cornelis Augustijn has remarked that a new attitude was emerging in the Germany of the 1960s in conferences on Reformation studies. Augustijn, who is associated with the Reformed tradition and holds a chair at the Vrije Universiteit in Amsterdam, recalled the 'old Erasmus' of Protestant scholarship as being, 'almost a Lutheran but lacking in courage.' This Erasmus, he says, was by then being replaced by a more individual and independent figure. At the same time Catholic scholars began to attend such conferences, the most distinguished among them being Erwin Iserloh, who was a pupil of Joseph Lortz, and Catholic interest in a reappraisal of the Reformation, and hence of Erasmus' place in it, gained great momentum in the wake of the Second Vatican Council.

As for the Protestants, prior to World War II German Lutheran scholarship, in Augustijn's view, had been interested only in Luther who was seen, as a theologian, 'to know all the questions and all of the answers,' a view that he thinks held out in some quarters until the 1970s. He also commends the influence of American Reformation scholarship, which added a social dimension and helped to eradicate the fixation on 'church history' in a narrow confessional mode. Augustijn himself did his doctoral work at the Vrije Universiteit. He intended at first to work on Bucer, but he concluded after reading Bucer's works of the 1530s that, 'it all started with Erasmus,' a view which he felt was confirmed in reading Calvinist theologians of the seventeenth century. The title of his doctoral thesis was, 'Erasmus and the Reformation.'

At this point the story returns to the city of Rotterdam. In 1958 Cornelis Reedijk, since 1953 Keeper of the Municipal Library at Rotterdam, succeeded his old patron Dr Kossmann as Director in charge of the Library and of its remarkable Erasmus collection. Within a year he was approached informally about a suitable commemoration of the fifth centenary of Erasmus' birth in 1469. Reedijk proposed to the President of the Historical Society of Rotterdam – 'Roterodamum' – two suggestions. A major exhibition to be held at the Boymans van Beuningen Museum, and secondly, investigation of the question, whether there was need for a new critical edition of the works of Erasmus and, if so, by what means such an edition might be brought into being. These suggestions were sent with several others to the then Burgomaster, Mr G.E. van Walsum, who supported both of Reedijk's proposals, and who in turn addressed himself to the Royal Netherlands Academy of Sciences and Letters with a request for advice. At the same time, Reedijk took up the matter with his old supervisor, Waszink, a member of the section of the Academy for humane letters, and Waszink recommended the proposal to the President, J.N. Bakhuizen van den Brink, who happened to be a close friend of the Burgomaster, van Walsum. The Royal Academy through its section for humane letters appointed a commission to formulate an appropriate response to the Burgomaster's request for advice, and the members of the commission were Bakhuizen van den Brink, R.R. Post, the historian of the *Devotio moderna*, J.H. Waszink and Cornelis Reedijk. It is perhaps not entirely surprising that this committee agreed about the need for a new critical edition, and recommended that it could only be achieved as a co-operative, international project undertaken by a team of scholars.

The Royal Academy endorsed these views and so informed the city of Rotterdam. The Academy was willing also to include the preparations for the edition among its current projects, and asked the International Union of Academies to lend its support, which it did. The city of Rotterdam agreed to supply facilities for whatever international meetings should prove necessary, and in the event, has paid for all subsequent meetings of the Council, including the travel costs of the participants. In commenting on this interesting series of developments Reedijk observed that, as a native son, he knew 'the Rotterdam way of doing business,' and that in taking these initiatives, he was also aware that, compared to other Dutch cities, Rotterdam was remarkable for its support of cultural activity. It is appropriate to recall that at an earlier time, the city of Rotterdam had contributed to the costs of the Leiden edition.

In December 1963, an international group of experts gathered in Rotterdam to discuss the practical measures needed. Among the participants was a distinguished scholar representing the International Union of Academies who gave the project his enthusiastic support: Roger Baskerville Mynors of Oxford. Others who participated were

J.N. Bakuizen van den Brink (Leiden, chairman), Léon-E. Halkin (Liège), Otto Herding (Münster), K.F. Kumaniecki (Warsaw), Pierre Mesnard (Tours), R.R. Post (Nijmegen), C. Reedijk (by now Director of the Royal Library at The Hague, honorary secretary), F. Schalk (Cologne), Antonio Vilanova (Barcelona), Christoph Vischer (Basel), and J.H. Waszink (Leiden). These participants laid the foundations concerning editorial policy and the organization of the work, and constituted themselves the International Council for the Edition of the Complete Works of Erasmus.[17]

Reedijk recalls that with the establishment of the *Conseil international* (as it is usually known) the project rather slipped to the margin of other priorities until the Dutch received a visit from a notable refugee scholar in America, Paul Oskar Kristeller. Reedijk then joined with Waszink and van den Brink to obtain a grant from the Academy to employ a permanent Secretary, and the person chosen was C.M. Bruehl. In due course an executive committee was established to carry on the daily work of the edition, and its personnel explain the four signatories to the General Introduction: Waszink, Reedijk, Halkin, and Bruehl.

The names of Kristeller, Reedijk, Halkin, and Bruehl return us to our opening theme of direct influence from survivors of the war. Halkin, who is now (1994) very aged, occupies a special place in the esteem of Dutch scholars as a committed Catholic who distinguished himself in the resistance, survived capture and brutal torture (including the notorious imprisonment known as 'Nacht und Nebel'), and who has carried ever since as a lasting memento a crippled right arm. His memoirs of those events – *A l'Ombre de la Mort* with a preface by François Mauriac – is a classic of wartime literature in Europe. Pierre Mesnard, another of the original members of the Conseil, brought out the first French translation of Erasmus' *De libero arbitrio* in Algiers in 1945, where he had served with the army of the Free French.

Clemens Bruehl had the most idiosyncratic history of all. In about 1938, he had been smuggled as a teenager from Berlin across the Dutch border by his Jewish parents and lived for a year or so on a farm with a Calvinist family. In the early years of the war he enroled at the University of Amsterdam, and lived in a sixteenth-century Hofje or hostel near the centre of the city at 385–95 Prinsengracht. The Hofje had been built and endowed by a well-to-do Catholic sugar trader as an alms-house for widows, and had served its foundational purpose ever since with the spiritual services of the Jesuit Order. At the outbreak of the war the Hofje was evacuated, and it was informally occupied by university students who were secretly involved in the resistance. Clemens Bruehl lived to the end of his days in the rooms where, during the war, an erect six-footer with blond hair and Nordic blue eyes, he was able with forged papers to pass as an officer in the Wehrmacht and ran an escape route for Jewish children, the last, perilous staging post of which was the Hofje. After the war, the Hofje became an official student residence of the University of Amsterdam, and the person put in charge was Clemens Bruehl. I well recall the evening when, removing a short series of shelves in his diminutive sitting-room, he pushed back a panel to reveal a hidden cupboard in which, as he said, 'you could hide three children.'

Historians must beware of assuming that a convergence of interests establishes a fact. It does not; but the circumstance that two of the four signatories of the General Introduction to the Amsterdam *Opera Omnia*, one a Catholic and the other a Jew, were men of unquestionable heroism during the German occupation, and a third, the moving spirit, had had his own experience of life in a concentration camp,[18] and had seen his university, famous for its Arminian and liberal traditions, closed down and his studies put in peril by the instruments of the same abysmal idiology – this circumstance is, I suggest, too important to escape remark. Nor can we neglect the part played by the city of Rotterdam. Ever loyal to the memory of its most famous son, it bore terrible scars from the ferocious and prolonged bombardment it received as a consequence of its being the largest port in Europe, a bombardment more severe than that inflicted on any other city in the Low Countries. In its corporate identity it was another tortured veteran of the destructive energies of war. Near the centre of Rotterdam there is a most remarkable sculpture commemorating its wartime holocaust. The city is personified as the ravaged figure of an angular, anguished woman gazing upwards, her outstretched arms twisted towards the heavens, her mouth open in a silent, endless scream. It is the most compelling monument to the cost of war that I have seen, and it was pointed out to me by the only German member of the original Council, Otto Herding.[19]

To recall Dom Germain's pleasure in his honorary degree at the University of Oxford, there are various ways of organizing a family of scholars. The Maurist Congregation was one; the collegiate society of Oxford and Cambridge another. Yet another was, I believe, the wartime experience of many of those who laid the foundations of ASD.

The story of the Toronto *Collected Works of Erasmus* is simpler, but forms a suitable epilogue to this initiative.[20] I have mentioned already the relevance of Canadian post-war interest in the humanities to the birth of CWE, but the actual initiative once again came from a single individual. In August 1968, R.M. Schoeffel, then editor for modern languages at University of Toronto Press, was moved to curiosity about why so few of the writings of an author as significant as Erasmus were available in English. Where, in the Netherlands, the role of North Holland Publishing Company followed on the Royal Dutch Academy's approval of the proposal for a new critical edition, in Toronto the initiative of a university press was all-important to the very conception of the project of an Englishing of Erasmus' works. In an atmosphere of collegial discussion and debate the idea won the support in principle of the managing editor Francess G. Halpenny, and of the editors for classics (Prudence Tracy) and humanities (Jean C. Jamieson). As a second step the opinions of local scholars in the University of Toronto were elicited, after which a second round of consultations were set in motion in North America and Europe. It became clear that there was considerable interest in the translation of more than the correspondence (the initial proposal), partly because of the growing accumulation of occasional translation, some of very doubtful quality.

In 1969 a chance meeting with Margaret Mann Phillips at a conference in New York allowed the present chronicler to canvass her support, and to discover that a more modest project concerning part of the correspondence had already elicited the interest of Sir Roger Mynors. Following a visit by the Director of the Press, Marsh Jeanneret, to Oxford, permission was granted by Clarendon Press to make full use of P.S. Allen's edition of the correspondence, and within the same year the Press secured the active adhesion and collaboration of two scholars whose reputations were of undoubted importance in lending this nascent and rather unlikely undertaking scholarly credibility internationally: the Canadian historian, Wallace K. Ferguson, and Sir Roger Mynors. In the same preparatory period, R.J. Schoeck of the University of Toronto had explored the interest of the American scholars Richard Sylvester and Myron Gilmore, and had opened discussions with Cornelis Reedijk, while D.F.S. Thomson, also of the University of Toronto, agreed to collaborate with Mynors in initiating the enterprise by translating Allen's *Epistolae*. It is also worthy of note that CWE was born in Toronto, where the university could supply extensive scholarly resources and where there was a well-established *de facto* ecumenical dimension born of the particular historical experience of Canada's largest Anglophone university.

By this time a warm response had been heard from scholarly voices at home and abroad. The names of S.L. Greenslade of Oxford, Roland Bainton and Richard Sylvester of Yale, Marcel Bataillon of the Collège de France, Myron Gilmore of Harvard, Werner Kaegi of Basel, and Margaret Mann Phillips, already mentioned, are representative. At the conference on Erasmus held in Rotterdam in 1969, direct contact was made with Cornelis Reedijk and the organizers of ASD, whose reaction from the first was friendly and positive. Liaison between CWE and ASD has been maintained from the start, initially by the presence of Craig R. Thompson on the Editorial Board of the former and Council of the latter, more recently by that of James McConica in the same roles, and by the addition of Joannes Trapman, Secretary to the Council of ASD, to the Editorial Board of CWE.

The aim of CWE, not a critical edition but a translation, is to bring the highest scholarly standards to the creation, annotation, and presentation of translated texts. This conception was tested with the appearance of the first volume of correspondence in 1974, in which the preliminary matter lists an editorial board headed by a 'Co-ordinating Editor,' who was R.J. Schoeck from 1968 to 1970, then Beatrice Corrigan, also of the University of Toronto.[21] There were two Literary Editors, R.A.B. Mynors and D.F.S. Thomson, and two Historical Editors, Wallace K. Ferguson and James Kelsey McConica. By the time the fourth volume of correspondence appeared, in 1977, the Editorial Board had been enlarged with the additions of Peter G. Bietenholz of the University of Saskatchewan, Paul F. Grendler of the University of Toronto, G.M. Story of the Memorial University of Newfoundland, and Craig R. Thompson of the University of Pennsylvania.

As something has been said already about the organization of CWE, two significant departures from the Dutch practice should here be made clear. The project would have been unthinkable for University of Toronto Press without the promise of financial support for research costs for the first five years of its existence by the Killam Fund of the (then) Canada Council, a funding body for support of the arts and humanities that came into existence as a result of the Massey Commission, referred to above.

A second distinctive feature is the close relation between CWE and the Press, which through an Executive Committee, maintains a working link with the Editorial Board. This link is maintained through the close working relationship between its Chairman, R.M. Schoeffel, and the Chairman of the Editorial Board, since 1975 James McConica. The Chairman of the Executive Committee is responsible for manuscripts after their arrival at the Press and for maintaining constant supervision over editing and production. The Chairman of the Editorial Board is responsible for direction of policy, recruitment, supervision of all work in progress, and in brief, the preparation of manuscripts. Regular meetings of the Editorial Board – originally semi-annual, later annual, and now biennial – provide the needed scholarly continuity and regular assessment of the work of CWE, each volume in preparation being assigned to one member of the Board for critical scrutiny, along with that of the Executive Assistant. The Executive Assistant, who for long was Erika Rummel, has the task particularly of insuring the fidelity of translations both with respect to the original Latin and to the general standard and aims of the series.

It is clear that the full extent of the project, originally estimated at forty volumes, will be nearer ninety, of which thirty-two have appeared to date (1994). The first volume was published in 1974, five years after the first volume of the Amsterdam *Opera omnia* appeared on its scheduled anniversary date, 1969. The two series together provide remarkable testimony to the effectiveness of scholarly collaboration in the late twentieth century, and to the lasting importance in our cultural and spiritual history of the figure who has inspired them. We must hope that resources will continue to be found to perpetuate these projects and to see them to completion.

NOTES

1 *Patristique et Antiquité tardive en Allemagne et en France de 1870 à 1930*, Actes du Colloque franco-allemand de Chantilly (25–7 octobre 1991) 165–90, in Collection des Études Augustiniennes, Série Moyen Age-Temps Modernes 27 (Paris 1993)
2 Ibid 165, no. 1
3 Ibid 168
4 Ibid 175
5 Ibid 173
6 Ibid 185; cf '... the spirit of the age in France, the appearance of a great legislator [Dom Didier de la Cour] followed by a succession of scholars of genius, and the acquisition of headquarters in the capital at a moment when Paris became, for the second time in her long history, the intellectual centre of Europe'; cf. David Knowles, 'The Maurists,' *Great Historical Enterprises* (London 1963) 38
7 Vessey, op cit 186; Betty Radice, ed. *Edward Gibbon, Memoirs of My Life* (Penguin Books 1984) 80
8 Vessey 188–9 and note 77

9 The omission of some shorter pieces prompted Wallace Ferguson to publish a supplement, *Erasmi Opuscula* (The Hague 1933).

10 H.M. Allen ed *Letters of P.S. Allen* (Oxford 1939) 11

11 P.S. Allen, Preface to *Opus Epistolarum Des. Erasmi Roterodami* vol i (Oxford 1906) v

12 Volume 10 appeared in 1941, volume 11 in 1947.

13 ASD I, 1 vii–xxi. See also the memoir by W.R.H. Koops, 'Cornelis Reedijk: een schets' in the Festschrift C. Reedijk, *Boek, Bibliotheek en geesteswetenschappen* (Hilversum 1986). Other personal information in what follows is based entirely on my conversations with colleagues in ASD, and with respect to C.M. Bruehl, on his direct testimony over several years.

14 A series of citations bearing on several aspects of a thesis

15 General Introduction, xv

16 Ibid xiv

17 Ibid xvi

18 In the winter of 1944, following the German offensive on the Ardennes salient and fearing the fall of Antwerp and the likelihood of another German draft of manpower for forced labour, Cornelis Reedijk and a friend attempted to escape to the liberated zones of Brabant by crossing the Rhine in a rowboat. They were captured and Reedijk, as the supposititious leader, was sentenced to be shot. This sentence was commuted, but both were sent for the remainder of the war to the concentration camp at Amersvoort.

19 It should be added that the director of North Holland Publishing Company, Mr M.D. Frank, himself a Jewish survivor of the war, undertook to publish the entire edition without subvention, an arrangement honoured by the successor company of Elsevier.

20 For a fuller account see J.K. McConica and R.M. Schoeffel, 'The Collected Works of Erasmus,' *Scholarly Publishing* (Toronto, July 1979) 313–24.

21 When Beatrice Corrigan was succeeded in turn by James McConica in 1975, the title too was changed to that of 'Chairman of the Editorial Board.'

MEMBERS OF THE CONFERENCE

Katherine Acheson, University of Toronto
Catherine Amadio, Wilfrid Laurier University
Megan Armstrong, University of Toronto
Mary Baldwin, University of Toronto Press
G.E. Bentley Jr, University of Toronto
Joseph Black, University of Toronto
Stephen Buick, University of Toronto
Rob Buranello, University of Toronto
James Carley, York University
Lisa Celovsky, University of Toronto
David Carlson, University of Ottawa
Viviana Comensoli, Wilfrid Laurier University
Judith Deitch, University of Toronto
Konrad Eisenbichler, University of Toronto
James Estes, University of Toronto
Charles Fantazzi, University of Windsor
James K. Farge, Pontifical Institute of Mediaeval Studies
Gillian Fenwick, University of Toronto
David Galbraith, University of Toronto
John N. Grant, University of Toronto
Francess G. Halpenny, University of Toronto
Jocelyn Hillgarth, Pontifical Institute of Mediaeval Studies
Ann M. Hutchison, Pontifical Institute of Mediaeval Studies
Robert M. Kingdon, University of Wisconsin–Madison
J. Daniel Kinney, University of Virginia
Christine Kralik, University of Toronto
Joyce Lorimer, Wilfrid Laurier University
Michael McClintock, University of Toronto
James K. McConica, All Souls College, Oxford
William McCuaig, University of Toronto
Joseph C. McLelland, McGill University
Randall McLeod, University of Toronto
D.E. Moggridge, University of Toronto
Chris Nighman, University of Toronto
Anne M. O'Donnell, Catholic University of America
Mechtilde O'Mara, St Michael's College, Toronto
Werner Packull, University of Waterloo
Suzanne Rancourt, University of Toronto Press
Dylan Reid, University of Toronto
Janet Ritch, University of Toronto

Erika Rummel, Wilfrid Laurier University
Ron Schoeffel, University of Toronto Press
Harry R. Secor, University of Toronto
Douglas F.S. Thomson, University of Toronto
Brent Vallee, Wilfrid Laurier University
Germaine Warkentin, University of Toronto
John Warkentin, York University

LIST OF PREVIOUS PUBLICATIONS

DATE

DEMCO 38-297